THE JOURNEY CONTINUES

●

How is this Haggadah Different?

The Journey Continues was created to answer the need for an Exodus story told in its fullness, in the voices of women as well as the voices of men. It incorporates questions posed by daughters as well as by sons and includes symbols, stories and *midrashim* that flow from women's reflections and analyses. Interweaving new and traditional texts, this is a document of an evolving Jewish tradition that is being transformed by women's perceptions and strengthened by women's songs. Created in an era when individual differences are increasingly being recognized as sources that strengthen community celebrations, this *haggadah* integrates diverse approaches to the Exodus story and the Passover experience. A vision of a better world in which freedom belongs to all people is reflected throughout the text.

The Journey Continues integrates a thorough knowledge of tradition with a deep commitment to modern sensitivities of diversity and inclusion. All Hebrew is transliterated and translated. The glossary, notes, and boxed directions explain every step of the *seder* ritual and clarify potentially unfamiliar terms.

The Journey Continues is designed to be used in communal settings as well as in the more intimate context of a home *seder*. The *haggadah* can be used comfortably in gatherings of women and men, in multi-generational groups of family and friends, in coeducational groups of teens and young adults and in gatherings of women. It can be used in its entirety or as a supplement to other *haggadot*.

Introduction

Passover is the holiday most celebrated by Jews. Across the world, in grand and humble spaces, families and friends gather each year to reenact the Jewish people's journey from slavery to freedom, from despair to hope, from spiritual degradation to praise for the Divine. Passover helps keep Judaism alive by reminding us to see ourselves as if we had personally come out of Egypt. By personalizing our exodus, we inscribe this journey on our hearts. We draw on its lessons of wandering and exile throughout the year. And the memories of discussions around the *seder* table strengthen our connection to our tradition and to one another.

When we open a *haggadah* that our families have used for years, the pages may be stuck together with *charoset*. *Matza* crumbs make tracks along the bindings, and wine stains decorate the pages on which the plagues are enumerated. The *haggadah*, the text of the *seder*, is a script of questions and answers. Based upon the order for telling the story prescribed in the second century *Mishnah*, the *haggadah* is a collection of biblical excerpts and ritual direction, supplemented and enhanced over the centuries with creative interpretations, poems, and songs. Like any time-honored teaching tool, the *haggadah* has been adapted by each generation and culture that has used it around the family table.

In the 1970s and 80s, many American Jews applied their sense of empowerment and entitlement to their practice of Judaism, creating alternatives to traditional communal institutions and traditional forms of Jewish worship. Many began experimenting with a wide range of new liturgies, including homemade *haggadot* (plural of *haggadah*). Original *haggadot* were crafted by women who recognized that the traditional *seder* text reflects an exclusively male rabbinic tradition. These women were intent on creating more inclusive texts. Others, distant from tradition, used the *seder* as a bridge to a deeper understanding of Judaism. By the early 1990s, women's *s'darim* (plural of *seder*) were celebrated in many places across America and Canada. Most were intimate affairs with liturgies created by and for a select group of celebrants. Others were open to the community.

In 1994, shortly after its founding, Ma'yan: The Jewish Women's Project of the Jewish Community Center on the Upper West Side of Manhattan welcomed women in the greater New York area to prepare for Passover with a ritual celebrating women's experiences. Over 200 attended that first *seder*, using a new *haggadah* prepared by an editorial group including cantors, rabbis, students, community leaders and writers. Since then, more than 2,000 women and men have attended Ma'yan's annual community feminist *s'darim*.

This *haggadah* represents the work of the editors over the past three years. It draws from the insights and decisions of the first Ma'yan *haggadah* and the experience of the Ma'yan *s'darim*, as well as the work of the editors of *We Were All There*, the *haggadah* of the American Jewish Congress Feminist Center in Los Angeles.

Over the years, in addition to community feminist *s'darim*, Ma'yan has offered workshops on preparing for and conducting inclusive home *s'darim*. Ma'yan has also held Passover music workshops to introduce participants to a range of *seder* music, from traditional to contemporary. The aim of these programs has been to enable participants to plan and facilitate *s'darim*, celebrating all of our ancestors, and acknowledging the contributions of all celebrants present at the *seder* table.

Theology and Blessings: What about God and God-language?

B'rachot are a special genre of prayers invented by the rabbis in the second and third centuries. In contemporary times, some Jews have recast and reformulated selected *b'rachot* as part of a larger process of liturgical reform. This *haggadah* reflects this process by formulating each *b'racha* three ways: in an alternative feminine Hebrew, described in the following paragraph; in the traditional Hebrew; and in gender neutral English. Our expression of *b'rachot*, in feminine as well as in masculine language, reflects how prayer and ritual can be

בצאת ישראל:

The Journey Continues

MA'YAN PASSOVER HAGGADAH

Edited by:
Tamara Cohen
Rabbi Sue Levi Elwell
Debbie Friedman
Ronnie M. Horn

enhanced by using a variety of names and images for God.

A traditional *b'racha* mentions God's name and, according to most authorities, God's Kingship. Our alternative *b'rachot* use an ancient name for God, יה *Ya*, a shortened form of יהוה YHWH, the name we do not pronounce. It comes from the root of the verb "to be," suggesting process and inter-relationship as opposed to the hierarchical relationship implied by the traditional *Adonai*. We have also reinterpreted the classical requirement of extolling God as King. To the people who first called God מֶלֶךְ הָעוֹלָם *Melech ha-Olam*, "King of the Universe," the metaphorical use of the term in connection with God put human sovereignty into perspective, while underscoring the absolute power of the Divine Monarch. In our new *b'rachot*, instead of calling on God as King, we invoke רוּחַ *Ruach*, God's spirit, a force beyond the power of nature or human whim. In Genesis, we read וְרוּחַ אֱלֹהִים מְרַחֶפֶת עַל פְּנֵי־הַמָּיִם *V'ruach Elohim m'rachefet al p'nei hamayim*, "God's spirit hovered over the face of the deep" (Genesis 1:2). The word רוּחַ *Ruach* is conjugated as feminine. Using a gender-neutral image which is rendered in the feminine form in gender-bound Hebrew enables us to see God's fullness encompassing both maleness and femaleness, mirroring the creation of both men and women בְּצֶלֶם אֱלֹהִים *b'tzelem Elohim*, in God's image (Genesis 1:27).

Because this *haggadah*'s *b'rachot* emerge from an attempt to draw closer to God, we have included the traditional formulations for those for whom new language and images may be impediments. We urge you to experiment, and we hope that the new *b'rachot* will provide you with an opportunity to think about and discuss your relationship to God, language, imagery and prayer.

Ritual Objects and Symbols

A traditional *seder* plate includes *karpas*, *maror*, *charoset*, *pesach*, and *beitza*, egg. Some also include *chazeret*, a second bitter herb, which is added to the Hillel sandwich. Jews from different parts of the world interpret these symbols in different ways. *Karpas* can include parsley as well as other greens and potatoes. *Maror* can be horseradish root or bitter lettuce. *Charoset* can be made from apples and nuts, dates and figs or apricots and almonds, depending on the recipe's country of origin and family traditions for preparing of this dense, sweet paste. The *Talmud* teaches that *pesach*, traditionally represented by a *zro'a,* a lamb or chicken bone, can be represented on the plates of vegetarians by a beet, which bleeds when it is cut (Tractate Pesachim 114b). Iranian Jews add a plate of scallions to the *seder* table, reminiscent of the onions that sustained the Israelites in Egypt (Numbers 11:5) and the whips of the Egyptian taskmasters.

In recent years Elijah's cup has been complemented at many *s'darim* by Miriam's cup, which is filled with spring water. The growing tradition of using a special ceremonial cup in honor of Miriam is linked to *midrashic* accounts of Miriam's Well, which moved with the Jews from place to place as our ancestors traversed the desert after the Exodus.

Many contemporary egalitarian and feminist *s'darim* also include an orange on each seder plate. All instructions in this *haggadah* are indicated with an orange 🍊 . The origin of this tradition is unclear. Earlier editions of the Ma'yan *haggadah* included a story about a Jewish feminist speaking in Florida who was challenged by a hostile listener claiming that women belong in positions of authority within Judaism just as much as an orange belongs on a *seder* plate. The speaker, according to the story, responded that, like an orange on a *seder* plate, women's participation in Judaism represents transformation, not transgression.

While this story continues to be told, a more complete history of the orange tradition has recently been revealed. Lesbian *haggadot* written in the late 1970s proposed adding a crust of bread to the *seder* plate. This symbol served as a defiant response to the claim that being a Jewish lesbian is like eating bread on Passover. While some Jewish feminists adopted this practice, others, offended by the inclusion of leaven on a *seder* plate, substituted an orange.[1]

There are two more ritual items that have become a part of Ma'yan *s'darim*: a *tzedaka* box and a tambourine. Because Ma'yan *s'darim* are held before the holiday, each participant is offered the opportunity to fulfill the *mitzva* of *tzedaka* during the course of the *seder* celebration. If your *seder* is held during the holiday and you do not handle money, you may use your *afikoman* reward as an opportunity to teach the value of *tzedaka*.

The tambourine offers children as well as adults an additional way to rejoice, by making music with the instrument with which Miriam led the Israelite women in dancing at the shores of the Red Sea (Exodus 15:20). The tambourine is used in this *haggadah* to designate songs.

Music of the Haggadah

The Journey Continues includes the words of new songs as well as the texts of traditional tunes. New songs, written by Debbie Friedman and by other contemporary composers, are integrated into the *haggadah* text. They include new renditions and interpretations of texts traditionally a part of the celebration, such as *Hallel*, the *Birkat haMazon*, and *B'chol Dor Vador*, as well as new songs that are becoming a part of many *seder* celebrations. Singing the songs of the *haggadah* can transform a *seder* experience and help participants connect with the text in a new way. In order to make the music accessible, Debbie Friedman has produced a recording of the music of *The Journey Continues* which includes every song, traditional and new, from this *haggadah*. Ordering information is inside the back cover.

Creating an Inclusive Home Seder

Ma'yan has created *The Journey to Freedom* because we believe that the *seder* can

---

[1] Alpert, Rebecca. *Like Bread on the Seder Plate: Jewish Lesbians and the Transformation of Tradition*. New York: Columbia University Press, 1997. pp 2-4.

present Judaism at its best – inclusive, accessible, welcoming to all and open to people with a variety of relationships to their Judaism. Using this *haggadah* will help you create such an experience. But a *haggadah* is only a text, and as much as a *seder* depends on the *haggadah* or *haggadot* used, it depends even more on who is around the table and the connections they make with the text and with one another.

Who is at the table

Today's families are rich and varied. They are multi-generational, including individuals related by birth, adoption and affection. Some are Jews by birth, some are Jews by choice, some come from other traditions, and some from no tradition at all. One way to ensure a rich *seder* experience is to include a range of ages and backgrounds around your table, welcoming visitors and those new to your community, and following the tradition of including individuals who otherwise might not attend a *seder*.

An inclusive *seder* welcomes everyone and invites participation from the beginning. Guests may be asked to contribute by sharing a treasured recipe, preparing parts of the meal, or making decisions about the liturgy. You may want to ask everyone who is invited to bring a question or a poem to contribute to the evening. When family members and friends share the responsibilities for this special event, no single individual need bear the weight of this communal celebration. One way to bring people together at the outset of the *seder* is to ask them to introduce themselves, sharing something about their past experiences of Passover. When each voice is acknowledged, the celebration can begin.

The table

An inclusive *seder* does not have to take place in the dining room. Choose a room in your home that can comfortably accommodate the diverse participants who will attend. Will parents of small children be able to be a part of the evening? Will children have access to play space in addition to their places at the table? Will older people be comfortable in their chairs? Will those who have special needs be able to participate fully?

While most families prefer to hold their *s'darim* around a large table, other families use several small tables. Some families begin their *seder* in a family room, with the *seder* plate, *matza*, salt water, wine and glasses. Only when they arrive at *Shulchan Oreich*, the main meal, does everyone gather around the main table.

More about the haggadah

You may choose to use *The Journey Continues* in its entirety, or choose particular portions that will enrich and enhance your family's celebration. Read through the *haggadah* in the weeks before your *seder* and decide which pieces will and won't work for your family. Think about how to "customize" a *seder* experience that will include everyone present. You will want to include the essential sections of the *haggadah*, which are listed in the *Kadeish/Urchatz* chant that appears on p. 8. The *Maggid* section should include what some call "the four tellings": the Four Questions, the Four Children, biblical verses and their *midrashic* interpretations, and an explanation of *pesach*, *matza* and *maror*.

As more Jews become fluent in Jewish traditions, many families are designing and producing their own supplements to, or versions of, the *haggadah*. Such *haggadot* draw on a rich range of sources, both historical and contemporary, and reflect the geographical origins, the travels and the studies of individual family members. Some families create their own *haggadah* every few years, cutting and pasting from published editions, adding drawings and sketches by various family members, or marking children's growth by including artwork, poems and interpretations of various portions of the Passover story.[2]

Leaders and Readers

The most successful *s'darim* reflect not only shared planning and execution but shared liturgical leadership. While one person might be the primary facilitator, every person at the table should have an opportunity to read, respond, and, if able, to take a turn leading the group. Thus, *The Journey Continues* designates "readers" instead of assigning parts to a leader and participants. To prepare yourself to act as *seder* facilitator, become familiar with the *haggadah* or *haggadot* to be used. Then you will be able to guide others and to open discussion at particular times during the course of the evening. You may wish to underscore the importance of certain sections, encourage particular readers for chosen parts, or move quickly through various sections. Some sections invite discussion. After the *Ha Lachma Anya*, those gathered might discuss their understanding of "Let All Who Are Hungry Come and Eat." After the Four Questions, encourage those present to ask their own questions. As an introduction to *Hallel*, one might ask, "What has given us joy this year?" When the text speaks of our ancestors' bondage and journeys, think about including stories of those who journeyed to freedom more recently. Remember: when insights and experiences of each person around the *seder* table are shared, we fulfill the challenge of "in every generation, each of us should see ourselves as if we, ourselves, had come out of Egypt."

When to hold your seder

Most home *s'darim* are held on the first and second nights of Passover. Some people celebrate with different individuals on each night. Some have traditions of using different tunes or *haggadot* on each of the first two nights. Some attend *s'darim* on nights one and two, and then [2]gather together again on the seventh or eighth night with a special focus.

---

[2] A fine resource on *haggadot* and general preparation for the holiday is Ira Steingroot's *Keeping Passover: Everything You Need to Know to Bring the Ancient Tradition to Life and Create Your Own Passover Celebration* New York: HarperSan Francisco, 1995. Also see *The Art of Jewish Living: The Passover Seder* by Ron Wolfson with Joel Lurie Grishaver, Federation of Jewish Men's Clubs, 1988.

Planning A Communal Women's Seder

Early feminist *s'darim* were organized and attended by women who wanted to use the metaphors of liberation to explore women's expanding roles in society and in Judaism. Feminist *haggadot* provided an opportunity for women's voices to become a part of the telling of the Passover story. Some celebrations grew and moved out of private homes and into more public spaces. Women who attended were delighted to discover that they could reclaim this essential celebration of the Jewish year and that the *seder* could provide an opportunity to share their own stories with other women. Today, women's *s'darim* are organized by members of Jewish women's groups, sisterhoods, those affiliated with traditionally secular Jewish organizations and coalitions of individuals who come together specifically to create a women's *seder*. Many of these *s'darim* welcome women and men, and particularly encourage young people to attend.

If you are thinking about planning a communal women's *seder*, *The Journey Continues* offers you an ideal text in its entirety or as a model for creating a text in your own community. For detailed information contact Ma'yan for a copy of our guide to creating communal women's seders.

Next Year in Jerusalem

In this *haggadah*, tradition and innovation sit comfortably together, both in the words of the text and in the theology that supports those words. As the editors have worked with the *haggadah* text over the years, our appreciation of the richness and depth of the traditional text has increased. Even as we have discovered narrow places within the interpretation and realization of the traditional *haggadah*, we have gained new respect for the rabbis' wisdom in combining themes and pedagogical techniques. *The Journey Continues* reflects our attempt to create a usable, lyrical document of integrity that invites new generations of women and men to celebrate "*z'man cheiruteinu*," our season of liberation.

We understand the Ma'yan *haggadah* and *s'darim* as an expression of a Judaism transformed by contemporary women's honest struggle with tradition. This *haggadah* is rooted in the belief that as more women discover the delight of preparing for and celebrating this holiday of journey and liberation, we reclaim an essential piece of our past and stake a claim to our shared future. The *haggadah* also enriches and renews Judaism by exposing men to the voices and experiences of women of the past and present.

The *seder* ends with a challenge: next year in Jerusalem. For Jews, Jerusalem is not only a city but a symbol of the heart and soul of our people. When we end our *seder*, we understand the yearning for Jerusalem as a yearning for a healed and renewed Judaism that fully honors Jewish women and men, respecting the humanity of all people.

B'DIKAT CHAMEITZ

בדיקת חמץ

searching for leaven : a new approach

B'dikat Chameitz is a ritual traditionally conducted on the night before the first seder. As all leaven producst are forbidden to be in one's possession during Passover, this ritual involves a symbolic search for leaven, with a candle and feather. The following new text can be recited at the beginning of a women's seder held before Pesach. Alternatively, you may want to gather the women of your household on the night before Pesach, at the conclusion of cleaning your house or kitchen, or right before the seder to read the following together.

". . . Rabbi Alexandri, on concluding his prayer, used to add the following: Sovereign of the Universe, it is known full well to You that our will is to perform Your will and what prevents us? The yeast in the dough and the subjection to foreign powers. May it be Your will to deliver us from their hand, so that we may return to perform the statutes of Your will with a perfect heart."

Brachot 17a

Reader: The yeast in the dough prevents us from doing Your will. The yeast in the dough.

Reader: The exhaustion of all the cleaning and cooking.

Reader: The exclusionary language.

Reader: The weight of history.

Reader: The utter absence of women.

Reader: The assumption that we weren't there. Had nothing to say.

Reader: All this we have carried with us.

Reader: The injustices and the silences.

Reader: Those we have heard and those we have not heard.

All: Let us gather all this togther like crumbs. Like *chameitz* we are ready to burn. Let us enter into this *seder* as if there is no more *chameitz* anywhere.

Reader: As if every woman had a voice and a name and a story and a pen.

Reader: As if God had forever delighted in the image of Herself in each and every one of us.

All: As if freedom had been ours always, fully - like an open sea.

Reader: Whether or not we clean our kitchens, sell or give away our bread, at this moment we gather to rid ourselves of the yeast in the dough – of all in our tradition that keeps us from You, from ourselves, from rejoicing among our people.

Reader: We gather here, before Pesach, to temporarily put aside the *chameitz* that will remain part of our lives and part of our struggles. In so doing we temporarily allow ourselves to taste true freedom.

If you have gathered a symbolic pile of chameitz *you may burn it after saying the following blessings. You may want to use the same flame to burn the* chameitz *for lighting the festival candles.*

בְּרוּכָה אַתְּ יָהּ אֱלֹהֵינוּ רוּחַ הָעוֹלָם אֲשֶׁר קִדְּשַׁתְנוּ בְּמִצְוֹתֶיהָ וְצִוַּתְנוּ עַל בִּעוּר חָמֵץ.

B'rucha At Ya Eloheinu Ruach ha-Olam asher kid'shatnu b'mitzvoteha v'tzivatnu
al biur chameitz.

or

בָּרוּךְ אַתָּה יי אֱלֹהֵינוּ מֶלֶךְ הָעוֹלָם אֲשֶׁר קִדְּשָׁנוּ בְּמִצְוֹתָיו וְצִוָּנוּ עַל בִּעוּר חָמֵץ.

Baruch Atah Adonai Eloheinu Melech ha-Olam asher kid'shanu b'mitzvotav v'tzivanu
al biur chameitz.

You are Blessed, O God, Spirit of the World, who makes us holy with *mitzvot* and
commands us to burn *chameitz*.

כָּל חֲמִירָא וַחֲמִיעָא דְּאִכָּא בִרְשׁוּתִי. דַּחֲמִיתֵהּ וּדְלָא חֲמִיתֵהּ. דְּבִעַרְתֵּהּ וּדְלָא בִעַרְתֵּהּ. לִבְטֵל וְלֶהֱוֵי הֶפְקֵר כְּעַפְרָא דְּאַרְעָא.

Kol chamira vachami'a d'ika virshuti. Dachamitei u-d'la chamitei. D'viartei u-d'la viartei.
Lib'teil v'lehevei hefkeir k'afra d'ara.

Every sort of *chameitz* in my possession, which I have seen or not seen, destroyed or not destroyed
let it be null and void, ownerless, like the dust of the earth.

Creating Holy Space

בְּרוּכוֹת הַבָּאוֹת תַּחַת כַּנְפֵי הַשְׁכִינָה

B'ruchot habaot tachat kanfei haSh'china

בְּרוּכִים הַבָּאִים תַּחַת כַּנְפֵי הַשְׁכִינָה

B'ruchim habaim tachat kanfei haSh'china

May you be blessed beneath the wings of Sh'china

Be blessed with love, be blessed with peace.

Reader: To the Temple in Jerusalem
our ancestors carried sheep and goats,
pomegranates and dates.

Reader: We are also ripe and burdened,
arms outstretched with gifts,
we carry our names, our histories, our memories and fears.

All: We have come here together to build something holy.
A makom kadosh, separate and apart.
We have come to rest, to sing and tell stories.
We have come to learn, to teach and to grow.
We bless this time with our presence.
We welcome God's Presence into our midst.

The time is now.

We've gathered 'round.

So bring all your gifts,

And bring all your burdens with you.

No need to hide.

Arms open wide.

We gather as one.

To make a makom kadosh.

We come to tell.

We come to hear.

We come to teach, to learn,

We come to grow.

And so we say,

The time is now.

Sing to the One.

God's Presence is here,

Sh'china, You will dwell among us.

We'll make this space

A holy place,

So separate, so whole,

Rejoice every soul

Who enters here.

Lighting the Candles

O hear my prayer,

I sing to You.

Be gracious to the ones I love,

And bless them with goodness, and mercy and peace,

O hear my prayer to You.

Let us light these lights,

And see the way to You,

And let us say: Amen.

Light the candles and recite blessings. Words in parentheses are added when the seder falls on Shabbat.

בְּרוּכָה אַתְּ יָהּ אֱלֹהֵינוּ רוּחַ הָעוֹלָם אֲשֶׁר קִדְּשַׁתְנוּ בְּמִצְוֹתֶיהָ
וְצִוַּתְנוּ לְהַדְלִיק נֵר שֶׁל [שַׁבָּת וְשֶׁל] יוֹם טוֹב:

B'rucha At Ya Eloheinu Ruach ha-Olam asher kid'shatnu b'mitzvoteha
v'tzivatnu l'hadlik neir shel (Shabat v'shel) Yom Tov.

or

בָּרוּךְ אַתָּה יי אֱלֹהֵינוּ מֶלֶךְ הָעוֹלָם אֲשֶׁר קִדְּשָׁנוּ בְּמִצְוֹתָיו
וְצִוָּנוּ לְהַדְלִיק נֵר שֶׁל [שַׁבָּת וְשֶׁל] יוֹם טוֹב:

Baruch Atah Adonai Eloheinu Melech ha-Olam asher kid'shanu b'mitzvotav
v'tzivanu l'hadlik neir shel (Shabat v'shel) Yom Tov.

You are Blessed, O God, Spirit of the World, who makes us holy with *mitzvot* and commands us
to kindle the light of (*Shabbat* and of) the festival day.

 Shehecheyanu, *the prayer for special occasions, is recited after this first blessing of the* seder.

בְּרוּכָה אַתְּ יָה אֱלֹהֵינוּ רוּחַ הָעוֹלָם שֶׁהֶחֱיָתְנוּ וְקִיְּמַתְנוּ וְהִגִּיעַתְנוּ לַזְּמַן הַזֶּה:
B'rucha At Ya Eloheinu Ruach ha-Olam
shehecheyatnu v'kiy'matnu v'higiatnu laz'man hazeh.

or

בָּרוּךְ אַתָּה יי אֱלֹהֵינוּ מֶלֶךְ הָעוֹלָם שֶׁהֶחֱיָנוּ וְקִיְּמָנוּ וְהִגִּיעָנוּ לַזְּמַן הַזֶּה:
Baruch Atah Adonai Eloheinu Melech ha-Olam
shehecheyanu v'kiy'manu v'higianu laz'man hazeh.

You are Blessed, Our God, Spirit of the World, who keeps us in life, who sustains us
and who enables us to reach this season.

Reader: For centuries, Jewish women have followed the blessing of the festival lights with a
t'chine, a private woman's prayer. Tonight we keep this tradition alive with the
words of this Sephardic *t'chine*:

Reader:

יְהִי רָצוֹן מִלְפָנַיִךְ יָה אֱלֹהַי וֵאלֹהֵי אֲבוֹתַי וְאִמּוֹתַי שֶׁתָּחֹנִּי אוֹתִי
Y'hi ratzon milfanayich, Ya Elohai veilohei avotai v'imotai shetachoni oti

וְאֶת מִשְׁפַּחְתִּי וְתִתְּנִי לָנוּ וּלְכָל יִשְׂרָאֵל חַיִּים טוֹבִים וַאֲרֻכִּים
v'et mishpachti v'tit'ni lanu ul'chol Yisraeil chayim tovim va-arukim

וְתִזְכְּרִינוּ בְּזִכָּרוֹן טוֹב וּבִבְרָכָה וְתִפְקְדִינוּ בִּפְקֻדַּת יְשׁוּעָה וְרַחֲמִים
v'tizk'rinu b'zikaron tov uviv'racha v'tifk'dinu bif'kudat y'shua v'rachamim

וּתְבָרְכִינוּ בְּרָכוֹת גְּדוֹלוֹת וְתַחֲזִיקִי בָּתֵּינוּ.
u't'varchinu b'rachot g'dolot v'tachziki bateinu.

Reader: May it be Your will, my God and God of my ancestors, to be gracious to me and to all my family and to give us, and all Israel, a good and long life. Remember us with goodness and blessing, and grant us salvation and mercy. Grant us abundant blessing, and fortify the places we call home.

Reader:

וְתַשְׁכִּינִי שְׁכִינָתֵךְ בֵּינֵינוּ בְּהֵאָסְפוּתֵינוּ כַּאן הָעֶרֶב.

V'tashkini sh'chinateich beineinu b'hei-asfuteinu kan ha'erev.

וּתְזַכֵּנוּ לְגַדֵּל יְלָדִים חֲכָמִים וּנְבוֹנִים אוֹהֲבֵי יָהּ

Ut'zakeinu l'gadeil y'ladim chachamim un'vonim, ohavei Ya,

יִרְאֵי אֱלֹהִים אַנְשֵׁי אֱמֶת וּמְפִיצֵי קֹדֶשׁ. מִי יִתֵּן וְתַלְמִידֵינוּ

yirei Elohim, anshei emet, um'fitzei kodesh. Mi yitein v'talmideinu

יָאִירוּ אֶת־הָעוֹלָם בַּתּוֹרָה וּבְמַעֲשִׂים טוֹבִים.

ya-iru et ha-Olam baTorah u'v'ma-asim tovim.

Reader: May Your Presence dwell among us as we gather here tonight. May we be blessed with wise and learned disciples and children, lovers of God who stand in awe of You, people who speak truth and spread holiness. May those we nurture light the world with *Torah* and good deeds.

Reader:

שִׁמְעִי אֶת־תְּחִנָתִי בָּעֵת הַזֹּאת בִּזְכוּת שָׂרָה וְרִבְקָה וְרָחֵל וְלֵאָה

Shim'i et t'chinati ba-eit hazot bizchut Sara v'Rivka v'Racheil v'Lei-a,

וּבִלְהָה וְזִלְפָּה אִמוֹתֵינוּ וְהָאִירִי אוֹר פָּנַיִךְ לְעוֹלָם וָעֶד

v'Bilha v'Zilpa, imoteinu v'ha-iri or panayich l'olam va'ed,

בְּאוֹר נֵרוֹתֵינוּ וְנִוָּשֵׁעָה. וְנֹאמַר אָמֵן.

b'or neiroteinu v'nivashei-a. V'nomar Amen.

Reader: Hear the prayers I utter now in the name of our mothers Sarah, Rebekah, Rachel and Leah, Bilhah and Zilpah. May Your light, reflected in these candles, surround us always. And let us say, Amen.

Miriam's Cup

 One person at the table lifts Miriam's Cup.

All: We begin our *seder* with *Kos Miryam*, Miriam's Cup. Legend tells of a mysterious well filled with *mayim hayyim*, living waters, that followed the Israelites through their wandering in the desert while Miriam was alive.

Reader: Miriam's Well was said to hold Divine power to heal and renew. Its fresh waters sustained our people as we were transformed from a generation shaped by slavery into a free nation. Throughout our subsequent journeys, we have sought to rediscover these living waters.

Reader: Tonight at our *seder*, let us remember that we are still on the journey. Just as the Holy One delivered Miriam and her people, just as they were sustained in the desert and transformed into a new people, so may we be delivered, sustained and transformed on our journey to a stronger sense of ourselves, both as individuals and as one people. May the Cup of Miriam refresh and inspire us as we embark on our journey through the *haggadah*.

 Miriam's Cup is now filled. Each individual pours water from her or his own water glass into Miriam's Cup.

All: זֹאת כּוֹס מִרְיָם, כּוֹס מַיִם חַיִּים. זֵכֶר לִיצִיאַת מִצְרָיִם:

Zot Kos Miryam, kos mayim chayim. Zeicher l'tzi-at Mitztrayim.

Reader: This is the Cup of Miriam, the cup of living waters. Let us remember the Exodus from Egypt.

Reader: These are the living waters, God's gift to Miriam, which gave new life to Israel as we struggled in the wilderness.

All: Blessed are You God, Who brings us from the narrows into the wilderness, sustains us with endless possibilities, and enables us to reach a new place.

The Journey to Freedom

Rav explained that Miriam had prophesied, "My mother is destined to give birth to a son who will save Israel from Egypt." And so, when Moses was born...the house, all of it, was flooded with radiant light. (Talmud Tractate Sotah 12b)

All: How does the journey to freedom begin?

Reader: Once, and then again and again. We wake and for the hundredth morning in a row, grope in the early silence for the words to describe what is wrong. One day, words begin. We are wrenched from the patterns that have defined our lives. We can no longer live as we have lived.

All: How does our people's journey begin?

Reader: In a hut where midwives work, Shifra turns to Pu'ah and sees in the spark of her partner's eye something she did not see the day before. Together they dare to defy Pharaoh, preserve life, ensure their people's future.

Reader: In the dark room where Yocheved labors to give birth, her daughter Miriam sits close by, humming a chant her grandmothers sang while mixing mortar. Suddenly she hears an infant's cry. And within her, hope rises like a new song. She sees beyond Egypt, to bright desert spaces and mountains, to far-off vineyards heavy with fruit.

All: How does the journey to freedom begin?

Reader: Once, and then again. In small, scattered, heroic acts and moments of vision until the humming rises and disparate voices come together into the cry of a people. "A long time after that the king of Egypt died, but the Israelites were still groaning under bondage, and their cry for help from the bondage rose up to God." (Exodus 2:23)

Where does the journey begin

Where will we go

Hours pass, the answers might change

As we keep moving along

Stand at the shores of the sea

Fearful, we want to turn back

The sea parts, our eyes fill with wonder

As we go along on our journey

Where does the journey begin

Where will we go

Days pass, the answers can change

As we keep moving along

Stepping into the unknown

Hear the echoes of Miriam's song

We awaken, retelling our stories

As we go along on our journey

Where does the journey begin

Where will we go

Years pass, the answers have changed

As we keep moving along

Cross the sea, it's the time

To sing a song, we are free

Dance with your timbrels in hand

There's no turning back from this journey

Where does the journey begin

Where will we go

Hours pass, the answers might change

As we keep moving along

Days pass, the answers can change

As we keep moving along

Years pass, the answers have changed

As we keep moving along.

A road map for our journey: the seder (order)

Blessing the Fruit of the Vine	*Kadeish*	קַדֵּשׁ
Washing the Hands	*Urchatz*	וּרְחַץ
Dipping the Greens	*Karpas*	כַּרְפַּס
Dividing the *Matza*	*Yachatz*	יַחַץ
Telling the Story	*Maggid*	מַגִּיד
Washing the Hands	*Rachtza*	רָחְצָה
Blessing the *Matza*	*Motzi Matza*	מוֹצִיא־מַצָּה
Eating the Bitter Herb	*Maror*	מָרוֹר
Hillel Sandwich	*Koreich*	כּוֹרֵךְ
The Festive Meal	*Shulchan Oreich*	שֻׁלְחָן עוֹרֵךְ
Finding the Hidden *Matza*	*Tzafun*	צָפוּן
Blessing After the Meal	*Bareich*	בָּרֵךְ
Giving Praise	*Hallel*	הַלֵּל
Concluding the *Seder*	*Nirtza*	נִרְצָה

KADEISH

קַדֵּשׁ

blessing the fruit of the vine

Reader: At every *seder* we drink four cups of wine linked to God's four promises to Israel.

All: As it is written, "I will bring you out from under the burdens of Egypt. I will deliver you from bondage. I will redeem you with an outstretched arm and great judgments. I will take you to be my people and I will be your God." (Exodus 6:6-7)

Reader: While *Pesach* has always been a celebration of God's fulfillment of these promises, we too have had a role in ensuring freedom. Our tradition recognizes the unique role of women as God's partners in the Exodus, stating "it was for the sake of the righteous women of that generation that we were redeemed from Egypt." (Sotah 9b) Since we understand redemption from Egypt as a constant historical process, we honor righteous women of every generation who have struggled for freedom.

Fill your first cup. For this cup and each of the others you may use the text provided or insert a biography from Appendix 1. Using historical figures from your own community and/or family can also be meaningful.

Reader: The first cup.

. . . וְהוֹצֵאתִי אֶתְכֶם מִתַּחַת סִבְלֹת מִצְרָיִם:

V'hotzeiti etchem mitachat sivlot Mitzrayim.

"...I will bring you out from under the burdens of Egypt." (Exodus 6:6)

Reader: Living at a time when Jews were fleeing the pogroms in Eastern Europe, the poet Emma Lazarus crafted an unforgettable image of a deliverer in her celebrated poem "The New Colossus." Speaking to Jews and all other immigrants to America, Lazarus' Mother of Exiles proclaims "Give me your tired, your poor/Your huddled masses yearning to breathe free."

Reader: These words which grace the pedestal of the Statue of Liberty were written by a woman born in New York City in 1849, the daughter of an Ashkenazi mother and Sephardic father whose families had been in America since colonial times. Comfortable in their American identity, Lazarus' parents gave her a secular education. Thus, as she explained in 1877, while her "interest and sympathies were loyal to [her] race. . . [her] religious convictions and the circumstances of [her] life" had led her to feel "somewhat apart from [her] people."

Moved by the plight of Russian Jews in the 1880s, Lazarus, already a published poet of acclaim and a member of the New York cultural elite, began to educate herself as a Jew. She published *Songs of a Semite*, a collection of poetry with Jewish themes. She wrote essays challenging her non-Jewish readers to reject their anti-semitism, while urging her Jewish audiences to join her in taking an active role in aiding immigrants to America and supporting the resettlement of Palestine.

Emma Lazarus' life was cut short tragically by cancer. She died at 38, but her words remain as a testament to her passionate embrace of and struggle with her multiple identities as a writer, a woman, an American and a Jew.

 Lift your glass for the blessing over the wine. Words in parentheses are added on Shabbat. The entire blessing in the feminine is followed with the traditional kiddush formulation.

(וַיְהִי־עֶרֶב וַיְהִי־בֹקֶר יוֹם הַשִּׁשִּׁי. וַיְכֻלּוּ הַשָּׁמַיִם וְהָאָרֶץ וְכָל־צְבָאָם. וַתְּכַל אֱלֹהִים בַּיּוֹם הַשְּׁבִיעִי מְלַאכְתָּהּ אֲשֶׁר עָשָׂתָה. וַתִּשְׁבֹּת בַּיּוֹם הַשְּׁבִיעִי מִכָּל־מְלַאכְתָּהּ אֲשֶׁר עָשָׂתָה. וַתְּבָרֶךְ אֱלֹהִים אֶת יוֹם הַשְּׁבִיעִי וַתְּקַדֵּשׁ אֹתוֹ, כִּי בוֹ שָׁבְתָה מִכָּל מְלַאכְתָּהּ אֲשֶׁר־בָּרְאָה אֱלֹהִים לַעֲשׂוֹת.)

בְּרוּכָה אַתְּ יָהּ אֱלֹהֵינוּ רוּחַ הָעוֹלָם בּוֹרֵאת פְּרִי הַגָּפֶן.

בְּרוּכָה אַתְּ יָהּ אֱלֹהֵינוּ רוּחַ הָעוֹלָם אֲשֶׁר בָּחֲרָה־בָּנוּ מִכָּל־עָם וְרוֹמְמַתְנוּ מִכָּל־לָשׁוֹן וְקִדְּשַׁתְנוּ בְּמִצְוֹתֶיהָ. וַתִּתְּנִי־לָנוּ, יָהּ אֱלֹהֵינוּ, בְּאַהֲבָה, (שַׁבָּתוֹת לִמְנוּחָה וּ) מוֹעֲדִים לְשִׂמְחָה, חַגִּים וּזְמַנִּים לְשָׂשׂוֹן, אֶת יוֹם (הַשַּׁבָּת הַזֶּה וְאֶת יוֹם) חַג הַמַּצּוֹת הַזֶּה, זְמַן חֵרוּתֵנוּ, (בְּאַהֲבָה) מִקְרָא קֹדֶשׁ, זֵכֶר לִיצִיאַת מִצְרָיִם. כִּי בָנוּ בָחַרְתְּ, וְאוֹתָנוּ קִדַּשְׁתְּ, מִכָּל־הָעַמִּים (וְשַׁבָּת) וּמוֹעֲדֵי קָדְשֵׁךְ (בְּאַהֲבָה וּבְרָצוֹן) בְּשִׂמְחָה וּבְשָׂשׂוֹן הִנְחַלְתָּנוּ. בְּרוּכָה אַתְּ יָהּ מְקַדֶּשֶׁת (הַשַּׁבָּת וְ) יִשְׂרָאֵל וְהַזְּמַנִּים.

(Vay'hi erev vay'hi voker yom hashishi. Vay'chulu hashamayim v'hararetz v'chol tz'va-am. Vat'chal Elohim bayom hash'vi-i m'lachta asher asta. Vatishbot bayom hash'vi-i mikol m'lachta asher asta. Vat'varech Elohim et yom hash'vi-i vat'kadeish oto, ki vo shavta mikol m'lachta asher bar'a Elohim la-asot.)

B'rucha At Ya Eloheinu Ruach ha-Olam boreit p'ri hagafen. B'rucha At Ya Eloheinu Ruach ha-Olam asher bachara vanu mikol am v'rom'matnu mikol lashon v'kid'shatnu b'mitzvoteiha. Vatit'ni lanu, Ya Eloheinu, b'ahava (Shabatot lim'nucha u-) moadim l'simcha, chagim uzmanim l'sason, et yom (haShabat hazeh v'et yom) chag hamatzot hazeh, z'man cheiruteinu, (b'ahava) mikra kodesh, zeicher litzi-at Mitzrayim. Ki vanu vachart, v'otanu kidasht, mikol ha-amim (v'Shabat) umo-adei kodsheich (b'ahava uv'ratzon) b'simcha uv'sason hinchalatnu. B'rucha At Ya m'kadeshet (haShabat v') Yisraeil v'haz'manim.

(וַיְהִי־עֶרֶב וַיְהִי־בֹקֶר יוֹם הַשִּׁשִּׁי. וַיְכֻלּוּ הַשָּׁמַיִם וְהָאָרֶץ וְכָל־צְבָאָם. וַיְכַל אֱלֹהִים בַּיּוֹם הַשְּׁבִיעִי מְלַאכְתּוֹ אֲשֶׁר עָשָׂה. וַיִּשְׁבֹּת בַּיּוֹם הַשְּׁבִיעִי מִכָּל־מְלַאכְתּוֹ אֲשֶׁר עָשָׂה. וַיְבָרֶךְ אֱלֹהִים אֶת יוֹם הַשְּׁבִיעִי וַיְקַדֵּשׁ אֹתוֹ, כִּי בוֹ שָׁבַת מִכָּל־מְלַאכְתּוֹ אֲשֶׁר־בָּרָא אֱלֹהִים לַעֲשׂוֹת.)

בָּרוּךְ אַתָּה יי אֱלֹהֵינוּ מֶלֶךְ הָעוֹלָם בּוֹרֵא פְּרִי הַגָּפֶן.

בָּרוּךְ אַתָּה יי אֱלֹהֵינוּ מֶלֶךְ הָעוֹלָם אֲשֶׁר בָּחַר־בָּנוּ מִכָּל־עָם וְרוֹמְמָנוּ מִכָּל־לָשׁוֹן וְקִדְּשָׁנוּ בְּמִצְוֹתָיו. וַתִּתֶּן־לָנוּ, יי אֱלֹהֵינוּ, בְּאַהֲבָה (שַׁבָּתוֹת לִמְנוּחָה וּ) מוֹעֲדִים לְשִׂמְחָה, חַגִּים וּזְמַנִּים לְשָׂשׂוֹן, אֶת יוֹם (הַשַּׁבָּת הַזֶּה וְאֶת יוֹם) חַג הַמַּצּוֹת הַזֶּה, זְמַן חֵרוּתֵנוּ, (בְּאַהֲבָה) מִקְרָא קֹדֶשׁ, זֵכֶר לִיצִיאַת מִצְרָיִם. כִּי בָנוּ בָחַרְתָּ, וְאוֹתָנוּ קִדַּשְׁתָּ, מִכָּל־הָעַמִּים (וְשַׁבָּת) וּמוֹעֲדֵי קָדְשֶׁךָ (בְּאַהֲבָה וּבְרָצוֹן) בְּשִׂמְחָה וּבְשָׂשׂוֹן הִנְחַלְתָּנוּ. בָּרוּךְ אַתָּה יי מְקַדֵּשׁ (הַשַּׁבָּת וְ) יִשְׂרָאֵל וְהַזְּמַנִּים.

(Vay'hi erev vay'hi voker yom hashishi. Vay'chulu hashamayim v'hararetz v'chol tz'va am. Vay'chal Elohim bayom hash'vi-i m'lachto asher asa. Vayishbot bayom hash'vi-i mikol m'lachto asher asa. Vay'varech Elohim et yom hash'vi-i vay'kadeish oto, ki vo shavat mikol m'lachto asher bara Elohim la-asot.)

Baruch Atah Adonai Eloheinu Melech ha-Olam borei p'ri hagafen.

Baruch Atah Adonai Eloheinu Melech ha-Olam asher bachar banu mikol am v'rom'manu mikol lashon v'kid'shanu b'mitzvotav. Vatiten lanu, Adonai Eloheinu, b'ahava (Shabatot limnucha u-) mo-adim l'simcha, chagim uz'manim l'sason, et yom (haShabat hazeh v'et yom) chag hamatzot hazeh, z'man cheiruteinu, (b'ahava) mikra kodesh, zeicher litzi-at Mitzrayim. Ki vanu vacharta, v'otanu kidashta, mikol ha-amim (v'Shabat) umo-adei kodsh'cha (b'ahava uv'ratzon) b'simcha uv'sason hinchaltanu. Baruch Atah Adonai m'kadeish (haShabat v') Yisraeil v'haz'manim.

(And it was evening and it was morning, the sixth day. Heaven, earth, and all hosts were finished. On the seventh day, God completed the work that had been done, and ceased upon the seventh day from all the work that had been done. God blessed the seventh day and made it holy. For on it God rested from all the work of creation that God had done.)

You are Blessed, Our God, Spirit of the World, who creates the fruit of the vine.

You are Blessed, Our God, Spirit of the World, who has chosen us and distinguished us by sanctifying us with the *mitzvot*. You have lovingly favored us with (*Shabbat* for rest and) festivals for joy, seasons and holidays for happiness, among them (this *Shabbat* and) this day of *Pesach*, the season of our liberation, a day of sacred assembly commemorating the Exodus from Egypt. You have chosen us, sanctifying us among all peoples by granting us (*Shabbat* and) Your sacred festivals (lovingly and gladly) in joy and happiness. You are Blessed, Our God, who sanctifies (*Shabbat* and) the people of Israel and the festival seasons.

Drink your first cup.

URCHATZ

•

ורחץ

washing of the hands

Wash your hands, using a pitcher or a cup, as a symbolic act of ritual cleansing. Everyone can wash or a representative may wash for the group. No blessing is recited.

KARPAS

•

כרפס

dipping of the greens

Reader: Long before the struggle upward begins,
there is tremor in the seed.
Self-protection cracks,
Roots reach down and grab hold.
The seed swells, and tender shoots push up toward light.
This is *karpas*: spring awakening growth.
A force so tough
It can break stone.

Reader: Dipping *karpas* into salt water, we recall the tears of our ancestors in bondage.

Reader: Dipping *karpas* into salt water, we call to mind the tears of an earth unable to fully renew itself this spring because of human neglect and greed.

Reader: Dipping *karpas* into salt water, we feel the sting of a society that refuses to celebrate the blossoming of women's bodies.

Reader: And why should salt water be touched by *karpas*?

All: To remind us that tears stop. Spring comes. And with it the potential for change.

Dip a vegetable into salt water. After the blessing, eat the karpas.

בְּרוּכָה אַתְּ יָהּ אֱלֹהֵינוּ רוּחַ הָעוֹלָם בּוֹרֵאת פְּרִי הָאֲדָמָה.

B'rucha At Ya Eloheinu Ruach ha-Olam boreit p'ri ha-adama.

or

בָּרוּךְ אַתָּה יי אֱלֹהֵינוּ מֶלֶךְ הָעוֹלָם בּוֹרֵא פְּרִי הָאֲדָמָה.

Baruch Atah Adonai Eloheinu Melech ha-Olam borei p'ri ha-adama.

You are Blessed, Our God, Spirit of the World, who creates the fruit of the earth.

YACHATZ

•

יחץ

breaking the middle matza

As we break the middle matza, we hide one portion. This hidden piece of matza, called the afikoman, must be found and shared at the end of the meal in order to complete the seder. The following is a kavana, an intention, reflecting one possible meaning for this symbolic act. The kavana can be followed by the Mi Shebeirach, based on the traditional prayer for healing.

Reader: Some do not get the chance to rise and spread out like golden loaves of *challah*, filled with sweet raisins and crowned with shiny braids.

Reader: Rushed, neglected, not kneaded by caring hands, we grow up afraid that any touch might cause a break. There are some ingredients we never receive.

Reader: Tonight, let us bless our cracked surfaces and sharp edges, unafraid to see our brittleness and brave enough to see our beauty.

Reader: Reaching for wholeness, let us piece together the parts of ourselves we have found and honor all that is still hidden.

Mi shebeirach avoteinu

M'kor Habracha l'imoteinu

May the Source of strength who blessed the ones before us,

Help us find the courage to make our lives a blessing

And let us say: Amen.

Mi shebeirach imoteinu

M'kor Habracha l'avoteinu

Bless those in need of healing with refua sh'leima,

The renewal of body, the renewal of spirit

And let us say: Amen.

MAGGID

•

telling the story

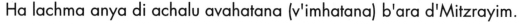

Turn down the covering of the matzot, showing the broken matza to everyone, then raise the seder plate.

All:

הָא לַחְמָא עַנְיָא דִי־אֲכָלוּ אֲבָהָתָנָא (וְאִמְהָתָנָא) בְּאַרְעָא דְמִצְרָיִם.

Ha lachma anya di achalu avahatana (v'imhatana) b'ara d'Mitzrayim.

כָּל־דִכְפִין יֵיתֵי וְיֵכוֹל.

Kol dichfin yeitei v'yeichol.

כָּל־דִצְרִיךְ יֵיתֵי וְיִפְסַח.

Kol ditzrich yeitei v'yifsach.

הָשַׁתָּא הָכָא. לְשָׁנָה הַבָּאָה בְּאַרְעָא דְיִשְׂרָאֵל.

Hashata hacha. L'shana haba-a b'ara d'Yisraeil.

הָשַׁתָּא עַבְדֵי. לְשָׁנָה הַבָּאָה בְּנֵי וּבְנוֹת חוֹרִין:

Hashata avdei. L'shana haba-a b'nei uv'not chorin.

Reader: In a language even the poorest would understand, our ancestors exiled in Babylonia used to proclaim:

All: This is the bread of affliction our ancestors ate in the land of Egypt. Let all who are hungry come and eat. Let all who are in need come and share our Passover. This year we are here. Next year in the land of Israel. This year we are slaves. Next year, may we all be free.

Reader: We, too, cry out the message.

Reader: *Ha lachma anya.* This is the taste of poverty all too familiar in America and worldwide.

Reader: *Di achalu avahatana.* We eat this bread of poverty and hardship even as we celebrate our freedom because as Jews, we must build sanctuaries with windows and doors that open to the world.

Reader: *Ha lachma anya.* Our country has the highest rate of children living in poverty in industrialized societies.

Reader: *Di achalu imhatana.* Our country has 20 million women living in poverty.

Reader: *Ha lachma anya.* Our country continues to allow more than two million people in need to live without homes.

Reader: *Kol dichfin yeitei v'yeichol.* Following the example of so many Jewish women who helped those less fortunate even when they themselves had little, we now renew our obligation to *tikkun ha-olam*, repair of the world, and commit to making *tzedaka* a greater part of our lives.

All: *Kol ditzrich yeitei v'yifsach.* Let all who are hungry come and eat.

This is a good point in the seder *to contribute, or discuss,* tzedaka. *While often translated as charity, the root of the Hebrew word* tzedaka *is justice.* Tzedaka *means using our resources to increase justice.*

The Four Questions

Reader: I learned the Four Questions in the kitchen. My mother handed me a towel and said: "I'll wash, you dry. I'll sing a few words, and you repeat." And so we sang, from the night after *Purim*, every night until I'd learned it all.

Reader: I taught the Four Questions at bath time to two little ones, lithe and slippery as seals. "I'll sing a few words, and then you sing," I said. They loved to dip and splash for "*sh'tei f'amim.*" And so we sang, from *Purim* to *Pesach*.
Every night, until they learned it all.

All: This is a rite of passage: learning our part, taking our turn.

Reader: Wine trembles in our cups. Candles flicker. Conversation stops. "And who will sing this year?" some grown-up asks.

All: We hear our names and—confident or not—begin to sing.

Fill your second cup and cover the three ceremonial matzot.

מַה־נִּשְׁתַּנָּה הַלַּיְלָה הַזֶּה מִכָּל־הַלֵּילוֹת?

Ma nishtana halaila hazeh mikol haleilot?

שֶׁבְּכָל־הַלֵּילוֹת אָנוּ אוֹכְלִין חָמֵץ וּמַצָּה. הַלַּיְלָה הַזֶּה כֻּלּוֹ מַצָּה:

Sheb'chol haleilot anu ochlin chameitz, umatza. Halaila hazeh kulo matza.

שֶׁבְּכָל־הַלֵּילוֹת אָנוּ אוֹכְלִין שְׁאָר יְרָקוֹת. הַלַּיְלָה הַזֶּה מָרוֹר:

Sheb'chol haleilot anu ochlin sh'ar y'rakot. Halaila hazeh maror.

שֶׁבְּכָל־הַלֵּילוֹת אֵין אָנוּ מַטְבִּילִין אֲפִילוּ פַּעַם אֶחָת. הַלַּיְלָה הַזֶּה שְׁתֵּי פְעָמִים:

Sheb'chol haleilot ein anu matbilin afilu pa-am echat. Halaila hazeh sh'tei f'amim.

שֶׁבְּכָל־הַלֵּילוֹת אָנוּ אוֹכְלִין בֵּין יוֹשְׁבִין וּבֵין מְסֻבִּין. הַלַּיְלָה הַזֶּה כֻּלָּנוּ מְסֻבִּין:

Sheb'chol haleilot anu ochlin bein yoshvin uvein m'subin. Halaila hazeh kulanu m'subin.

Why is this night different from all other nights? On all other nights we eat either *chameitz* or *matza*, but on this night, only *matza*. On all other nights we eat other kinds of vegetables, but on this night, *maror*. On all other nights we do not dip even once, but on this night, we dip twice. On all other nights we eat either sitting up or reclining, but on this night, we all recline.

Avadim Hayinu

Reader: "Only God" pulled my grandmother from the Cossack
Kept her from dying of nausea at sea,
And gave her the strength to climb
four flights of dark stairs on Rivington Street.

"There must be a God," my mother said,
Counting a live birth after many miscarriages
And the ten good years
between cancer and her death.

But God is not in my life story.
Until I remember that
"Our mothers and fathers were slaves in Egypt,"
And when they put down their tools
To walk for the rest of their lives
Under the desert sky,
They saw "God's mighty hand."
They knew "God's outstretched arm."

And so I unpack my grandmother's dishes every year
to tell the story of the Exodus from Egypt.

עֲבָדִים הָיִינוּ עַתָּה בְּנֵי חוֹרִין

Avadim hayinu. Ata b'nei chorin

We were slaves, now we are free.

Reader:

עֲבָדִים הָיִינוּ לְפַרְעֹה בְּמִצְרָיִם. וַתּוֹצִיאֵנוּ יָה מִשָּׁם בְּיָד חֲזָקָה וּבִזְרוֹעַ נְטוּיָה. וְאִלּוּ לֹא
הוֹצִיאָה מְקוֹר חַיֵּינוּ אֶת־אֲבוֹתֵינוּ וְאֶת־אִמּוֹתֵינוּ מִמִּצְרַיִם, הֲרֵי אָנוּ וְצֶאֱצָאֵינוּ, וְצֶאֱצָאֵי
עַמֵּנוּ מְשֻׁעְבָּדִים הָיִינוּ לְפַרְעֹה בְּמִצְרָיִם. וַאֲפִלּוּ כֻּלָּנוּ חֲכָמִים, כֻּלָּנוּ נְבוֹנִים, כֻּלָּנוּ זְקֵנִים,
כֻּלָּנוּ יוֹדְעִים אֶת־הַתּוֹרָה, מִצְוָה עָלֵינוּ לְסַפֵּר בִּיצִיאַת מִצְרָיִם. וְכָל הַמַּרְבֶּה לְסַפֵּר
בִּיצִיאַת מִצְרַיִם הֲרֵי זֶה מְשֻׁבָּח.

Avadim hayinu l'Pharoh b'Mitzrayim. Vatotzi–einu Ya misham b'yad chazaka uvizro-a
n'tuya. V'ilu lo hotzi-a M'kor Chayeinu et avoteinu v'et imoteinu miMitzrayim, harei anu
v'tze-etza-einu, v'tze-etza-ei ameinu m'shubadim hayinu l'Pharoh b'Mitzrayim. Va'afilu
kulanu chachamim, kulanu n'vonim, kulanu z'keinim, kulanu yod'im et haTorah, mitzva
aleinu l'sapeir bitzi-at Mitzrayim. V'chol hamarbeh l'sapeir bitzi-at Mitzrayim harei zeh
m'shubach.

All: We were slaves to Pharaoh in Egypt, and then God brought us out with a mighty
hand and an outstretched arm. But if God had not brought our ancestors out of
Egypt, we and our children and our children's children would still be enslaved to
Pharaoh in Egypt. So even if all of us were wise, all of us understanding, all of us
old, all of us learned in the *Torah*, it would still be a *mitzvah* for us to tell the story
of the Exodus from Egypt. And all who embellish the story deserve praise.

Ma-aseh • It Is Told. . .

Reader: In a traditional *seder*, we tell the story of sages in the second century who
gathered in B'nei B'rak to discuss the Exodus from Egypt. All were activists in the
struggle against Rome. They talked through the night until their students, standing

watch, alerted them with the words: *raboteinu, higi-a z'man*...The time has come to recite the morning *Sh'ma*. Tonight we remember the subversive courage of teachers of our own generation.

Reader: On *Rosh Chodesh Tevet* 5749 (1989), an extraordinary group of women from the United States and Israel, Canada and Great Britain, Brazil and West Germany, Argentina and South Africa, New Zealand and Sweden, 70 women strong, carried a *Sefer Torah* to the *Kotel*.

Reader: And they were so intent on praying together, Conservative women with Reform, Orthodox with Reconstructionist, so engrossed in the blending of separate voices and traditions, so at one with that sweet and holy sound, that they ignored the curses from beyond the *m'chitza*. They ignored the angry hands at their sleeves and the ugly words in their ears.

Reader: They formed a circle around the *Torah* and read from it aloud until the clear, bright syllables bounced against the ancient stones, shattered, recombined and echoed back across the Plaza, across Jerusalem: *Raboteinu, morateinu*, our rabbis and teachers. *Higi-a z'man*, it is time. *Raboteinu, achyoteinu*. Our rabbis and sisters, *higi-a z'man*....

The Four Daughters

Reader: The daughter in search of a usable past.
Ma hi omeret? What does she say?

Reader: "Why didn't the *Torah* count women among the '600,000 men on foot, aside from children' who came out of Egypt? And why did Moses say at Sinai, 'Go not near a woman,' addressing only men, as if preparation for Revelation was not meant for us, as well?"

Reader: Because she already understands that Jewish memory is essential to our identity, teach her that history is made by those who tell the tale. If *Torah* did not name and number women, it is up to her to fill the empty spaces of our holy texts.

Reader: And the daughter who wants to erase her difference. *Ma hi omeret*? What does she say?

Reader: "Can't one just be a Jew? Why must you keep pushing your women's questions into every text? And why are these women's issues so important to you?"

Reader: "To you," and "not to me." Since she so easily forgets the struggles of her mothers and sisters, you must set her teeth on edge by saying, "I thank God every morning for the blessing of being a woman."

Reader: And the daughter who does not know that she has a place at the table. *Ma hi omeref?* What does she say?

Reader: "What is this?"

Reader: Because she doesn't realize that her question is, in itself, a part of the *seder* tradition, teach her that the *haggadah* is an extended conversation about liberation, and tell her that her insights and questions are also text.

Reader: And the daughter who asks no questions.

Reader: You must say to her, "your questions, when they come, will liberate you from Egypt. This is how it is and has always been with your mothers and grandmothers. From the moment Miriam and the midwives questioned Pharaoh's edict until today, every question we ask helps us leave Egypt farther behind."

L'chi lach, to a land that I will show you

Leich l'cha, to a place you do not know

L'chi lach, on your journey I will bless you

And (you shall be a blessing) (3x) l'chi lach

L'chi lach, and I shall make your name great

Leich l'cha, and all shall praise your name

L'chi lach, to the place that I will show you

(L'simchat chayim) (3x) l'chi lach

And (you shall be a blessing) (3x) l'chi lach

Mit'chila • In the beginning

Reader: At first our mothers were like willows,
bowing earthward to the soil.
And then, they left their parents' homes,
loved wandering men, and followed them
under huge skies, charged with stars
and the slow progress of barren moons.

Our mothers measured time from month to month.
And when they conceived, carried, bore,
nursed, weaned, struggled for, fought for,
lost and wept for their children,
the stars answered with a laugh
and the wind with a promise.

And the slow moon followed
their children and children's children
down to Egypt, where they sojourned
and were later enslaved
and forced to bow earthward, to the soil.

Until, after 400 years, the promise was kept
and God drew them out of their narrow
confinement, and brought them out of Egypt
to follow the Covenant
under huge skies, charged with stars.

Tzei Ul'mad • Go Out and Study

In a traditional haggadah, "Go Out and Study" consists of an interplay between verses in Deuteronomy and rabbinic commentary on those verses. The following is a new commentary on one of the same verses.

Reader: וַיָּרֵעוּ אֹתָנוּ הַמִּצְרִים וַיְעַנּוּנוּ וַיִּתְּנוּ עָלֵינוּ עֲבֹדָה קָשָׁה:

Vayarei-u otanu haMitzrim va-y'anunu va-yitnu aleinu avoda kasha

Reader: "The Egyptians dealt harshly with us and mistreated us; they imposed hard labor on us." (Deuteronomy 26:6)

Reader: "And they mistreated us." What does this mean?

Reader: They mistreated us as it says, וַתְּעַנֶּהָ שָׂרַי, *Va-t'aneha Sarai*, "And Sarai mistreated her [Hagar]..." (Genesis, 16:6).

Reader: Why does the *Torah* use the same word for the mistreatment of the Israelites by the Egyptians as it uses for the mistreatment of Hagar the maidservant by her mistress Sarai? Surely the *Torah* understands that the mistreatment of an entire people in slavery is very different from the mistreatment of one woman by another.

Reader: This comes to teach us that, lest you think that you, as an Israelite, have no Pharaoh in you, remember that even your righteous foremother Sarai treated Hagar the Egyptian as the Egyptians treated our ancestors.

We follow our study of Torah with an adaptation of the traditional prayer for the completion of study.

For our teachers and their students
and the students of the students.
We ask for peace and loving kindness
and let us say: Amen.
And for those who study Torah, here and everywhere
May they be blessed with all they need.
And let us say: Amen.

The Ten Plagues

...The Holy One sat in judgement over the Egyptians and drowned them in the sea. In that instant, the ministering angels wished to sing before the Holy One, but God rebuked them, saying, "Those I have created with my own hands are drowning in the sea, and you utter song in my presence?" (Babylonian Talmud. Sanhedrin 39b)

Reader: We are about to recite the Ten Plagues. As we call out the words, we remove ten drops from our overflowing cups, not by tilting the cup and spilling some out, but with our fingers. This dipping is not food into food. It is personal and intimate, a momentary submersion like the first step into the Red Sea. Like entering a *mikvah*.

Reader: We will not partake of our *seder* feast until we undergo this symbolic purification, because our freedom was bought with the suffering of others.

Reader: As we packed our bags that last night in Egypt, the darkness was pierced with screams. Our doorposts were protected by a sign of blood. But from the windows of the Egyptians rose a slow stench: the death of their first born.

Reader: *Ya Sh'china*, soften our hearts and the hearts of our enemies. Help us to dream new paths to freedom.

Reader: So that the next sea-opening is not also a drowning; so that our singing is never again their wailing. So that our freedom leaves no one orphaned, childless, gasping for air.

At the recitation of each plague, we remove a drop of wine from our glasses, diminishing our joy because of the suffering of the Egyptians.

Blood	Dam	דָּם
Frogs	Tz'fardei-a	צְפַרְדֵּעַ
Lice	Kinim	כִּנִּים
Beasts	Arov	עָרוֹב
Cattle Disease	Dever	דֶּבֶר
Boils	Sh'chin	שְׁחִין
Hail	Barad	בָּרָד
Locusts	Arbeh	אַרְבֶּה
Darkness	Choshech	חֹשֶׁךְ
Slaying of the First Born	Makat B'chorot	מַכַּת בְּכוֹרוֹת

Reader: After the final plague, Pharaoh let the Israelites go. They left Egypt in the middle of the night, and with the full moon as their guide, they walked to the shores of the Red Sea.

Reader: According to one *midrash*, they continued to walk until the waters were up to their necks and then–a miracle! The waters parted, and the people crossed on dry land. As Moses and the people rejoiced in song, "...Miriam the Prophet, Aaron's sister, took a timbrel in her hand and all the women went after her with timbrels, dancing." (Exodus 15:20)

It has become a feminist seder tradition to dance with tambourines at this point in the haggadah.

CHORUS: And the women dancing with their timbrels

Followed Miriam as she sang her song.

Sing a song to the One whom we've exalted.

Miriam and the women danced and danced the whole night long.

And Miriam was a weaver of unique variety.

The tapestry she wove was one which sang our history.

With every thread and every strand she crafted her delight.

A woman touched with spirit, she dances toward the light.

(CHORUS)

As Miriam stood upon the shores and gazed across the sea,

The wonder of this miracle she soon came to believe.

Whoever thought the sea would part with an outstretched hand,

And we would pass to freedom, and march to the promised land.

(CHORUS)

And Miriam the Prophet took her timbrel in her hand,

And all the women followed her just as she had planned.

And Miriam raised her voice with song.

She sang with praise and might,

We've just lived through a miracle, we're going to dance tonight.

אִלּוּ הוֹצִיאָנוּ מִמִּצְרָיִם: דַּיֵּנוּ

Ilu hotzi-anu miMitzrayim. Dayeinu

אִלּוּ נָתַן לָנוּ אֶת הַשַּׁבָּת: דַּיֵּנוּ

Ilu natan lanu et haShabat. Dayeinu

אִלּוּ נָתַן לָנוּ אֶת הַתּוֹרָה: דַּיֵּנוּ

Ilu natan lanu et haTorah. Dayeinu.

Reader: It would have been enough for God to take us out of Egypt.

Reader: It would have been enough to bring us through the Red Sea, enough to give us the *Torah* and *Shabbat*, enough to bring us into the land of Israel.

Reader: While we count each of these blessings as if it would have been enough on its own, we know that more was given, and more is promised.

Reader: From singing *Dayeinu* we learn to celebrate each landmark on our people's journey. Yet we must never confuse these way stations with the redemptive destination. Because there is still so much to do in our work of repairing the world.

All: If we speak truthfully about the pain, joys and contradictions of our lives,

If we listen to others with sensitivity and compassion,

If we challenge the absence of women in traditional texts, chronicles of Jewish history and in the leadership of our institutions, *Dayeinu*.

If we continue to organize, march and vote to affirm our values,

If we fight economic injustice, sexism, racism and homophobia,

If we volunteer our time and money, *Dayeinu*.

If we break the silence about violence against women and children in the Jewish community and everywhere,

If we teach our students and children to pursue justice with all their strength,

If we care for the earth and its future as responsibly as we care for those we love,

If we create art, music, dance and literature, *Dayeinu*.

If we realize our power to effect change,

If we bring holiness into our lives, homes and communities,

If we honor our visions more than our fears, *Dayeinu*.

Pesach, Matza, Maror

Reader: According to Rabban Gamliel, one of our earliest rabbis, those who did not mention three things on Passover did not fulfill the obligation to tell the story: *pesach*, *matza* and *maror*.

We do not raise the pesach on the seder plate because it symbolizes a sacrifice that is no longer offered.

Reader: The *pesach* which our ancestors ate while the Temple still stood. Why did they eat it?

Reader: Because God passed over (*pasach*) the houses of the Israelites in Egypt while smiting the first born of every Egyptian family.

Raise the matza.

Reader: The *matza*, why do we eat this unleavened bread?

Reader: Because there was not enough time for our ancestors' dough to rise so they had to bake their unleavened dough into *matza* in the desert.

Raise the maror.

Reader: The *maror*, why do we eat these bitter herbs?

Reader: Because the Egyptians embittered the Israelites' lives.

Reader: Each of these three things, *pesach*, *matza* and *maror*, symbolize aspects of the Passover story. Yet displaying and explaining them does not necessarily ensure the completion of a *seder*.

All: We therefore add to Rabban Gamliel's list that no *seder* can be complete without the questions of daughters as well as sons and the memory of our mothers as well as our fathers. Thus, we sing, "In every generation all of us are obligated to see ourselves as though we personally left Egypt."

בְּכָל־דּוֹר וָדוֹר חַיָּבִים אָנוּ לִרְאוֹת אֶת־עַצְמֵנוּ כְּאִלּוּ

B'chol dor vador chayavim anu lirot et atzmeinu k'ilu

כְּאִלּוּ יָצָאנוּ

k'ilu yatzanu (3x)

מִמִּצְרַיִם

miMitzrayim.

In every generation each of us is obligated to see ourselves as if we left Egypt.

All:

לְפִיכָךְ אֲנַחְנוּ חַיָּבִים לְהוֹדוֹת לְהַלֵּל לְשַׁבֵּחַ לְפָאֵר לְרוֹמֵם לְהַדֵּר לְבָרֵךְ לְעַלֵּה וּלְקַלֵּס לְמִי שֶׁעָשָׂה לַאֲבוֹתֵינוּ וּלְאִמּוֹתֵינוּ וְלָנוּ אֶת־כָּל־הַנִּסִּים הָאֵלֶּה. הוֹצִיאָנוּ מֵעַבְדוּת לְחֵרוּת מִיָּגוֹן לְשִׂמְחָה מֵאֵבֶל לְיוֹם טוֹב וּמֵאֲפֵלָה לְאוֹר גָּדוֹל וּמִשְׁעְבּוּד לִגְאֻלָּה. וְנֹאמַר לְפָנָיו שִׁירָה חֲדָשָׁה. הַלְלוּיָהּ:

L'fichach anachnu chayavim l'hodot l'haleil l'shabei-ach l'fa-eir l'romeim l'hadeir l'vareich l'alei ul'kaleis l'mi she-asa la-avoteinu ul'imoteinu v'lanu et kol hanisim ha-eileh. Hotzi-anu mei-avdut l'cheirut, miyagon l'simcha, mei-eivel l'yom tov, umei-afeila l'or gadol, umishibud lig'ula. V'nomar l'fanav shira chadasha. Hal'lu-ya.

Therefore we rejoice in our obligation to thank, sing songs of praise, glorify, exalt, honor, bless, extol, and lift our voices to the One who is the Source of miracles for our ancestors and for us. God brought us forth from slavery to freedom, from sorrow to joy, from mourning to celebration, from darkness to great light, from bondage to redemption. Let us sing a new song. Halleluyah.

Hallel • Giving Praise
Psalm 114

בְּצֵאת יִשְׂרָאֵל מִמִּצְרָיִם בֵּית יַעֲקֹב מֵעַם לֹעֵז:

B'tzeit Yisraeil miMitzrayim beit Ya-akov mei-am lo-eiz.

הָיְתָה יְהוּדָה לְקָדְשׁוֹ יִשְׂרָאֵל מַמְשְׁלוֹתָיו:

Hay'ta Y'huda l'kodsho Yisraeil mamsh'lotav.

הַיָּם רָאָה וַיָּנֹס הַיַּרְדֵּן יִסֹּב לְאָחוֹר:

Hayam ra-a vayanos haYardein yisov l'achor.

הֶהָרִים רָקְדוּ כְאֵילִים גְּבָעוֹת כִּבְנֵי־צֹאן:

Heharim rak'du ch'eilim g'va-ot kivnei tzon.

מַה־לְּךָ הַיָּם כִּי תָנוּס הַיַּרְדֵּן תִּסֹּב לְאָחוֹר:

Ma l'cha hayam ki tanus haYardein tisov l'achor.

הֶהָרִים תִּרְקְדוּ כְאֵילִים גְּבָעוֹת כִּבְנֵי־צֹאן:

Heharim tirk'du ch'eilim g'va-ot kivnei tzon.

מִלִּפְנֵי אָדוֹן חוּלִי אָרֶץ מִלִּפְנֵי אֱלוֹהַּ יַעֲקֹב:

Milifnei adon chuli aretz milifnei Elo-ah Ya-akov.

הַהֹפְכִי הַצּוּר אֲגַם־מָיִם חַלָּמִישׁ לְמַעְיְנוֹ מָיִם:

Hahofchi hatzur agam mayim chalamish l'may'no mayim.

When Israel went out of Egypt, when the house of Jacob emerged from a babel of tongues, Judah became God's dwelling place, Israel, God's dominion. The sea looked and fled, the Jordan turned back. The mountains danced like lambs, the hills like young sheep. Why do you flee, O sea? O Jordan, why do you change your course? Why do you frolic, O mountains? Why do the hills tremble? In God's presence, the earth moves before the God of Jacob. You transform rocks into pools of water, You turn flint into flowing springs.

Second Cup

Reader: The second cup.

"וְהִצַּלְתִּי אֶתְכֶם מֵעֲבֹדָתָם"

"V'hitzalti etchem mei-avodatam"

"I will deliver you from under their bondage." (Exodus 6:6)

All: With this cup, we honor Hannah Greenebaum Solomon, the visionary leader who founded of the National Council of Jewish Women, the first national Jewish women's organization in this country.

Reader: Hannah Greenebaum Solomon was born in Chicago on January 14, 1858, the fourth of ten children. By the time she was chosen to organize the Jewish Women's Congress at the 1893 World's Columbian Exposition in Chicago, Solomon was a prominent leader in secular women's circles and in the Jewish community. It was at the close of this historic event that The National Council of Jewish Women was founded with the goal of promoting social justice, Jewish education and philanthropy. Solomon was unanimously chosen as its first president.

In the next decades, Solomon worked through the NCJW to provide women with Jewish education, unprecedented opportunities for leadership and avenues for helping immigrants. Solomon also founded Chicago's Bureau of Personal Service, which along with NCJW, pioneered social service programs before the establishment of a coordinated Jewish philanthropic effort in Chicago. A friend and colleague of Susan B. Anthony and Jane Addams, Solomon was a an outspoken advocate for women's suffrage and women's rights worldwide and the founder of a girls' school in Chicago. Solomon was also a proud liberal Jew, the first woman to speak from many pulpits in America. Wife, mother, grandmother and great grandmother, Solomon modeled a life in which extensive community involvement coexisted with a deep commitment to family.

All:

בְּרוּכָה אַתְּ יָה אֱלֹהֵינוּ רוּחַ הָעוֹלָם בּוֹרֵאת פְּרִי הַגָּפֶן.

B'rucha At Ya Eloheinu Ruach ha-Olam boreit p'ri hagafen.

or

בָּרוּךְ אַתָּה יי אֱלֹהֵינוּ מֶלֶךְ הָעוֹלָם בּוֹרֵא פְּרִי הַגָּפֶן.

Baruch Atah Adonai Eloheinu Melech ha-Olam borei p'ri hagafen.

You are Blessed, Our God, Spirit of the World, who creates the fruit of the vine.

Drink the second cup.

 RACHTZA

●

רחצה

washing of the hands

We wash our hands again, this time with a blessing. Because the act of washing is linked to the act of eating, we do not speak until after the second matza blessings.

בְּרוּכָה אַתְּ יָה אֱלֹהֵינוּ רוּחַ הָעוֹלָם
אֲשֶׁר קִדְּשַׁתָּנוּ בְּמִצְוֹתֶיהָ וְצִוַּתְנוּ עַל נְטִילַת יָדָיִם:

B'rucha At Ya Eloheinu Ruach ha-Olam
asher kidshatnu b'mitzvoteha v'tzivatnu al n'tilat yadayim.

or

בָּרוּךְ אַתָּה יי אֱלֹהֵינוּ מֶלֶךְ הָעוֹלָם
אֲשֶׁר קִדְּשָׁנוּ בְּמִצְוֹתָיו וְצִוָּנוּ עַל נְטִילַת יָדָיִם:

Baruch Atah Adonai Eloheinu Melech ha-Olam
asher kidshanu b'mitzvotav v'tzivanu al n'tilat yadayim.

You are Blessed, Our God, Spirit of the World,
who makes us holy with *mitzvot* and commands us to wash our hands.

MOTZI MATZA

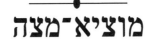 

מוֹצִיא־מַצָּה

blessing the matza

Raise the top and bottom matzot, and say the blessing, a reminder that matza is a form of bread.

בְּרוּכָה אַתְּ יָהּ אֱלֹהֵינוּ רוּחַ הָעוֹלָם הַמּוֹצִיאָה לֶחֶם מִן הָאָרֶץ.

B'rucha At Ya Eloheinu Ruach ha-Olam hamotzi-a lechem min ha-aretz.

or

בָּרוּךְ אַתָּה יי אֱלֹהֵינוּ מֶלֶךְ הָעוֹלָם הַמּוֹצִיא לֶחֶם מִן הָאָרֶץ.

Baruch Atah Adonai Eloheinu Melech ha-Olam hamotzi lechem min ha-aretz.

You are Blessed, Our God, Spirit of the World, who brings forth bread from the earth.

Put down the bottom matza, lift the broken middle one with the top one, and say the matza blessing.

בְּרוּכָה אַתְּ יָהּ אֱלֹהֵינוּ רוּחַ הָעוֹלָם אֲשֶׁר קִדְּשַׁתְנוּ בְּמִצְוֹתֶיהָ וְצִוַּתְנוּ עַל אֲכִילַת מַצָּה:

B'rucha At Ya Eloheinu Ruach ha-Olam
asher kidshatnu b'mitzvoteha v'tzivatnu al achilat matza.

or

בָּרוּךְ אַתָּה יי אֱלֹהֵינוּ מֶלֶךְ הָעוֹלָם אֲשֶׁר קִדְּשָׁנוּ בְּמִצְוֹתָיו וְצִוָּנוּ עַל אֲכִילַת מַצָּה:

Baruch Atah Adonai Eloheinu Melech ha-Olam
asher kidshanu b'mitzvotav v'tzivanu al achilat matza.

You are Blessed, Our God, Spirit of the World,
who makes us holy with *mitzvot* and commands us to eat *matza*.

MAROR

מרור
bitter herbs

Reader: This is the way to experience bitterness: take a big chunk of raw horseradish, let the burning turn your face all red.

Reader: This is the way to experience bitterness: dig back to a time of raw wounds, remember how it felt before the healing began, years or months or days ago.

Reader: This is the way to experience bitterness: hold the hand of a friend in pain, listen to her story, remember Naomi who renamed herself *Mara*, bitterness, because she "went away full but God brought [her] back empty." (Ruth 1:21)

Reader: How big a piece of *maror* do I have to eat to fulfill my obligation? And what if I've known enough pain this year already? And what if I eat the whole root and my tongue catches on fire and my ears burn? Then will I know slavery?

בְּרוּכָה אַתְּ יָהּ אֱלֹהֵינוּ רוּחַ הָעוֹלָם
אֲשֶׁר קִדְּשַׁתְנוּ בְּמִצְוֹתֶיהָ וְצִוַּתְנוּ עַל אֲכִילַת מָרוֹר:

B'rucha At Ya Eloheinu Ruach ha-Olam
asher kid'shatnu b'mitzvoteha v'tzivatnu al achilat maror.

or

בָּרוּךְ אַתָּה יי אֱלֹהֵינוּ מֶלֶךְ הָעוֹלָם אֲשֶׁר קִדְּשָׁנוּ בְּמִצְוֹתָיו וְצִוָּנוּ עַל אֲכִילַת מָרוֹר:

Baruch Atah Adonai Eloheinu Melech ha-Olam
asher kid'shanu b'mitzvotav v'tzivanu al achilat maror.

You are Blessed, Our God, Spirit of the World,
who makes us holy with *mitzvot* and commands us to eat bitter herbs.

Eat the maror *but do not recline because* maror *is a symbol of slavery.*

KOREICH
כּוֹרֵךְ
Hillel Sandwich

We now take some maror and charoset, put them between two pieces of matza and give the sandwich to the person on our left. In doing this, we recall our second century sage Hillel who, in remembrance of the loss of the Temple, created the Koreich sandwich. We also acknowledge how the presence of others helps us to move from bitterness to a healing engagement with community.

SHULCHAN OREICH
שׁוּלְחָן עוֹרֵךְ
The Festive Meal

In many Ashkenazi homes it is customary to begin the meal with hard-boiled eggs, usually dipped in salt water. The egg is rich with symbolic meaning, representing the renewal of spring and the cycle that brings us back, year after year, to the seder table. The roasted egg is also a reminder of the sacrifice which took place in the ancient Temple.

TZAFUN
צָפוּן
Retrieving the Hidden Matza

Reader: "So, who has found the *afikoman*?" we ask. The finders hold the napkin-covered *matza* tightly in their hands and are determined to bargain.

Reader: It's a part of our lesson plan–this small rebellion. Each year we teach a new generation to resist bondage, to envision someplace better, to savor freedom, and to take responsibility for the journeys of their lives.

Reader: And each year with the *afikoman* ritual, they hold power in their hands, just long enough to say, "Yes" or "No," with all eyes on them. With people waiting.

Reader: "We can't finish the *seder* without it."

Reader: ...Just long enough to learn to ask for what they want.

The afikoman is *distributed*. Each person eats a small piece as a sign that the meal has concluded.

BAREICH
•
ברך
Blessing After the Meal

The third cup is poured.

שִׁיר הַמַּעֲלוֹת בְּשׁוּב יי אֶת־שִׁיבַת צִיּוֹן הָיִינוּ כְּחֹלְמִים. אָז יִמָּלֵא שְׂחוֹק פִּינוּ וּלְשׁוֹנֵנוּ
רִנָּה. אָז יֹאמְרוּ בַגּוֹיִם הִגְדִּיל יי לַעֲשׂוֹת עִם־אֵלֶּה. הִגְדִּיל יי לַעֲשׂוֹת עִמָּנוּ, הָיִינוּ
שְׂמֵחִים. שׁוּבָה יי אֶת־שְׁבִיתֵנוּ כַּאֲפִיקִים בַּנֶּגֶב. הַזֹּרְעִים בְּדִמְעָה בְּרִנָּה יִקְצֹרוּ. הָלוֹךְ יֵלֵךְ
וּבָכֹה נֹשֵׂא מֶשֶׁךְ־הַזָּרַע בֹּא־יָבֹא בְרִנָּה נֹשֵׂא אֲלֻמֹּתָיו.

Shir hama-alot, b'shuv Adonai et shivat Tzi-yon, hayinu k'cholmim. Az yimalei s'çhok
pinu ulshoneinu rina. Az yomru vagoyim, hig'dil Adonai la-asot im eileh. Hig'dil Adonai
la-asot imanu hayinu s'meichim. Shuva Adonai et sh'viteinu ka-afikim banegev. Hazor'im
b'dim'a b'rina yik'tzoru. Haloch yei-leich uvacho nosei meshech hazara bo yavo v'rina
nosei alumotav.

A Song of Ascents. When God restores the scattered ones of Zion, it will be the fulfillment of a
dream. Our mouths will be filled with laughter then; our tongues with song. Then the nations will
say: "God has done great things for them." God has done great things for us. We rejoice.
Carry our captives back, O God, like water coursing through a dry riverbed. Those who sow in
tears will reap in joy. Those who plant in sorrow will return with song, sheaves piled high.

The following adaptation of the traditional Grace After Meals incorporates all the themes and many of the
core phrases of the traditional Hebrew blessings.

We bless You God

You have nourished all the world

With goodness, graciousness and kindness

May You give food and life to every living thing

May we all learn to do the same

And so we thank the One

Who gives us food for life
May we provide for every living soul
Baruch atah Adonai hazan et hakol

We thank You, God, for the legacy we share
For the rich.fertile land that we inherit
For the gift of freedom, of Torah, and of life
Every day, every season, every hour
You give us food to live
You give us strength to give
Every day, every moment with b'racha
Nodeh Lach, nodeh L'cha
We say toda raba
B'chol eit uv'chol sha-a

Kakatuv, *it is written in Torah*
You will eat, you will drink and you'll be sated
Then you will bless the One
Who has given you this world
Who has filled it with beauty and with life
We'll guard this earth, these lands
The torrent seas and sands
All the seeds that we have not yet sown
For land so rich and full
We give our thanks to You
Al haaretz v'al hamazon

O You, the God of our present and our past
Please remember those who came before us
And care for us as we pray for Y'rushalayim
The city of wholeness and peace

We ask that we be blessed

With everything that's good

That every blessing make our lives more whole

That every one of us

Be strengthened by Your light

Bakol, mi-kol, kol, kol

O, Source of compassion,

Through the ages we've been blessed

May we build this city of peace

And may all people make it a place of peace and freedom

In our day, now, the time has come

We bless the Source of all

Who builds Jerusalem

With compassion in our day

Boneh b'rachamav Y'rushalayim Amen

We bless You, O God, who has taught us what is good

Heiteev, meiteev, yeiteev

You have sustained us and blessed us now and at all times

Chein vachesed v'rachamim

Harachaman, *Your love surrounds us now and forever more.*

Harachaman, *bring truth and justice to Heaven and to Earth.*

Harachaman, *all generations will glorify and praise You.*

Harachaman, *You give us honor, may we live with dignity.*

Harachaman, *You give us freedom, may we help those imprisoned.*

Harachaman, *here at this table, we nourish one and all.*

Harachaman, *bless us with vision, a better world we promise.*

Harachaman, *the One of Mercy, be with us, Harachaman.*

(on Shabbat:)   Harachaman, *the One of Mercy, You give rest and comfort.*

Harachaman, *the One of Mercy, from now to eternity.*

(on holidays:)   Harachaman, *the One of Mercy, You give us days of goodness.*
Harachaman, *the One of Mercy, You give us sacred times.*

Oseh shalom bimromav hu ya-seh shalom
Aleinu v'al kol Yisraeil, v'al kol yoshvei teiveil, v'im-ru Amen.

Third Cup

Reader: The third cup.

וְגָאַלְתִּי אֶתְכֶם בִּזְרוֹעַ נְטוּיָה וּבִשְׁפָטִים גְּדֹלִים

V'ga-alti etchem bizro-a n'tuya uvish'fatim g'dolim

"And I will redeem you with an outstretched arm and with great judgments." (Exodus 6:6)

All: This cup is dedicated to Justine Wise Polier, a visionary family court judge and committed social activist who, with her own outstretched arms and great judgments, aided countless disadvantaged children in New York City and beyond.

Reader: Justine Wise Polier was born in 1903 to Rabbi Stephen Wise and Louise Waterman Wise, parents who raised her to embrace her responsibility to social justice as a Jew and an American. Throughout her college and law school years, she became increasingly involved in helping workers unionize. She aided strikers

in the Passaic textile mills throughout the 1920s. Sworn in as a justice of New York's Domestic Relations Court in 1935, Justine Wise Polier espoused an activist concept of the law. She pioneered the establishment of mental health, educational, and other rehabilitative services for troubled children. She also took a leading role in opposing racial and religious discrimination in public and private facilities.

As a committed Jewish leader, Justine Wise Polier spoke out against anti-semitism, urging Jews to lead the battle for human rights for all minorities. Together with her husband, Polier shaped the American Jewish Congress' policy on many progressive issues. After she retired from the bench, Polier continued to work on behalf of disadvantaged children through the Wiltwyck Home and School for Boys, the Citizens Committee for Children and the Children's Defense Fund.

All: בְּרוּכָה אַתְּ יָהּ אֱלֹהֵינוּ רוּחַ הָעוֹלָם בּוֹרֵאת פְּרִי הַגָּפֶן.

B'rucha At Ya Eloheinu Ruach ha-Olam boreit p'ri hagafen.

or

בָּרוּךְ אַתָּה יי אֱלֹהֵינוּ מֶלֶךְ הָעוֹלָם בּוֹרֵא פְּרִי הַגָּפֶן.

Baruch Atah Adonai Eloheinu Melech ha-Olam borei p'ri hagafen.

You are Blessed, Our God, Spirit of the World, who creates the fruit of the vine.

Drink the third cup and then fill the fourth cup.

Sh'foch Chamat'cha/Elijah's Cup

Reader: At this point in the *seder* Jewish communities, beset by persecution during the Crusades, opened their doors and recited the angry plea *"Sh'foch Chamat'cha...Pour out Your wrath upon the nations who do not know You."*

Reader: In other communities during the same period, the hope for redemption was so intense that they sang to invoke the Prophet Elijah who, according to legend, would herald an era of Messianic peace, justice and healing.

All: We open our doors now with the need to act on both impulses. The crimes of humanity that we continue to see—the rape and torture of innocents, ethnic cleansing, the destruction of entire cities and cultures—cry out for just retribution beyond our limited capacity. And our longing for peace, for healing of earth, body and spirit, still brings the hope-drenched melody of *Eiliyahu Hanavi* to our lips.

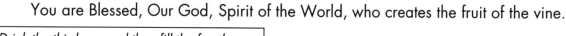

אֵלִיָּהוּ הַנָּבִיא, אֵלִיָּהוּ הַתִּשְׁבִּי, אֵלִיָּהוּ הַגִּלְעָדִי

Eiliyahu hanavi, Eiliyahu hatishbi, Eiliyahu hagiladi.

בִּמְהֵרָה בְיָמֵינוּ, יָבוֹא אֵלֵינוּ עִם מָשִׁיחַ בֶּן דָּוִד:

Bimheira v'yameinu, yavo eileinu, im mashiach ben David.

Elijah the Prophet, come to us soon, for you herald Messianic days.

Continue in the same melody, connecting the memory of Miriam the Prophet to that of Elijah.

מִרְיָם הַנְּבִיאָה, עֹז וְזִמְרָה בְּיָדָהּ.

Mir'yam han'vi-a oz v'zimra b'yada

מִרְיָם תִּרְקוֹד אִתָּנוּ, לְהַגְדִּיל זִמְרַת עוֹלָם.

Mir'yam, tirkod itanu, l'hagdil zimrat olam.

מִרְיָם תִּרְקוֹד אִתָּנוּ, לְתַקֵּן אֶת־הָעוֹלָם.

Mir'yam, tirkod itanu, l'takein et ha-olam

בִּמְהֵרָה בְיָמֵנוּ (הִיא) תְּבִיאֵנוּ, אֵל מֵי הַיְשׁוּעָה, אֵל מֵי הַיְשׁוּעָה:

Bim'heira v'yameinu, (hi) t'vi-einu. El mei ha-y'shua. El mei ha-y'shua.

Miriam the Prophet, strength and song are in her hand. Miriam will dance with us to strengthen the world's song. Miriam will dance with us to heal the world. Soon, and in our time, she will lead us to the waters of salvation.

HALLEL

◆

הלל

Giving Praise

Reader: We have invoked a redemptive future we cannot yet see, and now we sing toward that future with songs of praise.

Psalm 118: 1-2, 5

הוֹדוּ לַיי כִּי־טוֹב כִּי לְעוֹלָם חַסְדּוֹ: יֹאמַר־נָא יִשְׂרָאֵל כִּי לְעוֹלָם חַסְדּוֹ:

Hodu ladonai ki tov ki l'olam chasdo. Yomar na Yisraeil, ki l'olam chasdo.

Let all who revere God's name now say, "Ki l'olam chasdo"

Sing Praise to the One, for God is good, "Ki l'olam chasdo"

מִן־הַמֵּצַר קָרָאתִי יָּה עָנָנִי בַמֶּרְחָב יָה:

Min hameitzar karati Ya anani vamerchav Ya

From a narrow place, I cried out to God. God answered me with wide expanse.

An Additional song of praise: Psalm 150

הַלְלוּיָהּ. הַלְלוּ אֵל־בְּקָדְשׁוֹ, הַלְלוּהוּ בִּרְקִיעַ עֻזּוֹ:

Hal'lu-ya. Hal'lu eil b'kodsho, hal'luhu birki-a uzo.

הַלְלוּהוּ בִגְבוּרֹתָיו, הַלְלוּהוּ כְּרֹב גֻּדְלוֹ:

Hal'luhu bigvurotav, hal'luhu k'rov gud'lo.

הַלְלוּהוּ בְּתֵקַע שׁוֹפָר, הַלְלוּהוּ בְּנֵבֶל וְכִנּוֹר:

Hal'luhu b'teika shofar, hal'luhu b'neivel v'chinor.

הַלְלוּהוּ בְּתֹף וּמָחוֹל, הַלְלוּהוּ בְּמִנִּים וְעֻגָב:

Hal'luhu b'tof umachol, hal'luhu b'minim v'ugav

הַלְלוּהוּ בְּצִלְצְלֵי־שָׁמַע, הַלְלוּהוּ בְּצִלְצְלֵי תְרוּעָה:

Hal'luhu b'tziltz'lei shama, hal'luhu b'tziltz'lei t'rua,

כֹּל הַנְּשָׁמָה תְּהַלֵּל יָה. כֹּל הַנְּשָׁמָה תְּהַלֵּל יָה. הַלְלוּ־יָהּ:

Kol han'shama t'haleil ya. Kol han'shama t'haleil ya. Hal'lu-ya.

Halleluyah! Praise God in God's sanctuary; Praise God whose power the heavens proclaim. Praise God for mighty acts; Praise God for surpassing greatness. Praise God with shofar blast; Praise God with harp and lute. Praise God with drum and dance; Praise God with strings and pipe. Praise God with cymbals sounding; Praise God with cymbals resounding. Let every soul praise God. Halleluyah!

> On the second night of Passover we begin counting the Omer (a Biblically ordained grain offering).
> The Omer marks the fifty days between the second night of Passover and the first night of Shavuot.
>
> בְּרוּכָה אַתְּ יָהּ אֱלֹהֵינוּ רוּחַ הָעוֹלָם אֲשֶׁר קִדְּשָׁתְנוּ בְּמִצְוֹתֶיהָ וְצִוַּתְנוּ עַל סְפִירַת הָעֹמֶר:
> B'rucha At Ya Eloheinu Ruach ha-Olam asher kid'shatnu b'mitzvoteha v'tzivatnu al s'firat ha-omer.
>
> *or*
>
> בָּרוּךְ אַתָּה יי אֱלֹהֵינוּ מֶלֶךְ הָעוֹלָם אֲשֶׁר קִדְּשָׁנוּ בְּמִצְוֹתָיו וְצִוָּנוּ עַל סְפִירַת הָעֹמֶר:
> Baruch Atah Adonai Eloheinu Melech ha-Olam asher kid'shanu b'mitzvotav v'tzivanu al s'firat ha-omer.
> You are blessed, Our God, Spirit of the World, who makes us holy with *mitzvot*
> and commands us to count the *omer*.
>
> הַיּוֹם יוֹם אֶחָד לָעֹמֶר.
> Hayom yom echad la-omer.
> This day is Day One of the *Omer*.

Fourth Cup

Reader: Our fourth and final cup.

"וְלָקַחְתִּי אֶתְכֶם לִי לְעָם וְהָיִיתִי לָכֶם לֵאלֹהִים"

V'lakachti etchem li l'am v'hayiti lachem leilohim.

"And I will take you to be my people and I will be your God." (Exodus 6:7)

All: We raise this cup to honor Bella Abzug, the first Jewish woman to be elected to the United States Congress, a founding Second Wave feminist and a fighter for justice until her last breath.

Fiercely committed to *tikkun olam*, Abzug participated in some of the first women's seders, lending her humor, passion and *chutzpa* to the development of this ritual.

Reader: Born a month before American women won the right to vote, Bella Savitzy Abzug grew up in the Bronx, where as a young Zionist activist, she raised money by giving impassioned speeches at subway stops. After her father's death, Bella, a thirteen-year-old, challenged her traditional synagogue by reciting *Kadish* daily.

A graduate of Hunter College and Columbia Law School, Abzug defended victims of racial and ideological discrimination. In the 1960s, she helped found Women's Strike for Peace which protested war and nuclear proliferation. At the age of 50, running with the slogan "Woman's Place is in the House," Abzug became the first Jewish woman elected to the House of Representatives. She served three terms in Congress, introducing and writing important legislation on behalf of women, civil liberties and gays and lesbians. Abzug eventually brought her energy and principles to the world stage, founding the Women's Environmental Development Organization to help transform the United Nation's agenda on women, human rights and the environment. Inspiring generations of young women activists, Bella Abzug showed the world that a Jewish woman who speaks her mind and fights the fight really can make a difference.

בְּרוּכָה אַתְּ יָהּ אֱלֹהֵינוּ רוּחַ הָעוֹלָם בּוֹרֵאת פְּרִי הַגָּפֶן.

B'rucha At Ya Eloheinu Ruach ha-Olam boreit p'ri hagafen.

or

בָּרוּךְ אַתָּה יי אֱלֹהֵינוּ מֶלֶךְ הָעוֹלָם בּוֹרֵא פְּרִי הַגָּפֶן.

Baruch Atah Adonai Eloheinu Melech ha-Olam borei p'ri hagafen.

You are Blessed, Our God, Spirit of the World, who creates the fruit of the vine.

Drink the fourth cup.

NIRTZA

נרצה

Concluding the Seder

Reader: For hundreds of years, seders have concluded with words: "Next year in a rebuilt Jerusalem."

Reader: Jerusalem. A name that means city of peace, integrity, wholeness.

Reader: Jerusalem. A city of walls, ancient and new. Walls built of apricot Jerusalem stone. Walls built of misunderstanding, hatred, and violence between religious and secular, Jew and Arab, woman and man.

Reader: Jerusalem, what is our hope for your rebuilding?

All: May it be a year of building equality and inclusiveness.

May it be a year of building wholeness for our people.

May it be a year of building peace for all the peoples who sing to Jerusalem.

לְשָׁנָה הַבָּאָה בִּירוּשָׁלָיִם

L'shana haba-a bi-Y'rushalayim

Next year in Jerusalem.

All: How does the journey to freedom continue?

Reader: Following fire and cloud, we stumble, shivering with cold and fear.

Reader: Some will always cry out for Egypt, longing to return to the known.

All: How does the journey to freedom continue?

Reader: Risking together what we never imagined possible on our own, we keep walking. The sea rises to our nostrils. Then, with a breath, the waters part.

All: How does the journey to freedom continue?

Reader: We build fragile shelters and watch as they sway in the wind. Aching for song, our throats are parched. The water is too bitter to drink. Even *manna* sometimes tastes like sand.

All: But ours is a holy journey. We falter but will not turn back. Embracing the challenge of tradition, we clear new paths to the future. Ours is a holy journey, a journey towards new song.

May we be blessed as we go on our way,

May we be guided in peace,

May we be blessed with health and joy,

May this be our blessing, Amen.

May we be sheltered by the wings of peace,

May we be kept in safety and in love,

May grace and compassion find their way to every soul,

May this be our blessing, Amen.

Each year that you use this haggadah you can substitute different historical figures for the Four Cups. In this way you will be continually adding to your familiarity with women in Jewish history. The following biographical sketches, listed in alpabetical order, are taken from earlier editions of the Ma'yan haggadah.

Rachel Auerbach (1903 - 1976)

We honor Rachel Auerbach. Rachel Auerbach was a graduate in philosophy from Lwow University, a Polish Zionist and a literary modernist. She was one of the very few Jewish women before the Second World War to cross the gender barrier to acknowledged and respected artistic expression. When the war broke out in Poland, Auerbach was trapped in the Warsaw Ghetto. She devoted herself to writing stories and essays for the *Oneg Shabbos* project, which created a secret ghetto archive, parts of which were retrieved after the war. She also lectured for the ghetto's "popular university," and directed a soup kitchen on Kovno Street, where she tried to keep as many Jews as possible from starving to death. After the ghetto was destroyed, Rachel Auerbach continued to write from a hiding place on the Aryan side. After the war, Rachel Auerbach immigrated to Israel where she helped found *Yad Vashem*, Israel's Holocaust Memorial. She organized the Department for Collecting Witness Accounts and continued to chronicle life in Warsaw before the war. She died in Israel in 1976.

Roskies, David. *Literature of Destruction. Philadelphia*: Jewish Publication Society, 1992.

Asenath bat Samuel Barazani (1590 - 1670)

We honor Asenath bat Samuel Barazani, who lived in Kurdistan from 1590 until 1670. Born into a family of scholars, Asenath was educated to study and teach Torah. When she married, her *ketubah* included an unheard of stipulation exempting her from housework so that she could devote herself to study. When Asenath's husband died, she took over his position as the head of the academy that her father Samuel had established, and she became the primary teacher, preacher, interpreter of Jewish law, and fund-raiser for the seminary in Mosul. Her correspondence, written in a precise hand in elegant Hebrew, reveals poetic ability, scholarship, and a clear sense of the urgency of her mission. A traditional woman throughout her life, she trained her son Samuel to carry on the legacy of his grandfather and father, and he became a rabbi and teacher in Baghdad. Asenath's legacy is one of rare honor. A letter to her in 1664 declared, "My lady, my mother, my rabbanit...We are always ready to revere you and serve you truly and faithfully, but please do not forget [to mention] us in your prayers, for surely your prayer is more accepted [by God] and is equal to peace offerings, ascending to high heaven and binding the upper worlds with the earthly one."

Henry, S. and Taitz, E. *Written Out of History: Our Jewish Foremothers*. Fresh Meadows: Biblio Press, 1983; Sabar, Yona. *The Folk Literature of the Kurdistani Jews: An Anthology*. New Haven: Yale University Press, 1982.

Judith Kaplan Eisenstein (1910 - 1996)

With this cup we honor the memory of Judith Kaplan Eisenstein. In 1922, when Judith Kaplan was twelve years old she made history when she was called to the *Torah* as the first *Bat Mitzvah* by her father, Rabbi Mordecai Kaplan. This early experience served her well when, after earning bachelor and masters degrees in music at Columbia University, she became one of the few women to teach at the Jewish Theological Seminary. Her book of children's music, *Gateway to Jewish Song*, and her *Heritage of Jewish Music* quickly became classics. In 1934 she married her father's closest disciple, Rabbi Ira Eisenstein, who collaborated with her on some of the seven Jewish cantatas that she wrote during her career. While in her 50s, after raising her family, she earned a doctorate in Sacred Music at Hebrew Union College-Jewish Institute of Religion. She continued teaching rabbis and teachers at Hebrew Union College and at the Reconstructionist Rabbinical College, which her husband founded in 1968. Kaplan Eisenstein's life work reflected her belief that the rich legacy of Jewish music opens the way to the Jewish soul and to a deeper understanding of Jewish history.

Debra Nussbaum Cohen, "The First Bat Mitzvah Dies at the age of 86," *Daily News Bulletin of the Jewish Telegraphic Agency*, February 16, 1996.

Glikl of Hameln (1646-1724)

With this cup, we honor Glikl bas Judah Leib and Beila, more commonly known as Glückel of Hameln. Born in 1646 in the German town of Hamburg, Glikl's brief childhood was marked by dislocation due to the expulsion of Jews from her birthplace. By the age of twelve she was betrothed to Haim of Hameln, a young man she had never met but would grow to love deeply over the thirty years of their marriage. Glikl became a partner in all aspects of Haim's affairs, making business decisions, overseeing finances and drawing up contracts. As their business grew, so did their family. Glikl survived fourteen pregnancies and raised twelve children to adulthood. A tragic accident in 1689 killed Haim, taking from Glikl "the crown of [her] life." Laden with grief, financial burdens and a challenge to her faith in God, she assumed full responsibility for the family enterprise, travelling to business fairs throughout Western Europe, opening her own stocking factory and store, and skillfully arranging her children's marriages. She also began a project that would claim her a role in history: she began to write her memoirs. Glikl's memoirs invite the reader into the heart and mind of a seventeenth century Jewish woman. Her stories and descriptions of everyday life reflect a keen intelligence and devout piety while providing a window on the spiritual and material reality of Jewish life in pre-modern Europe. We bless this cup of wine in memory of Glikl. We celebrate the vision, creativity and confidence which led her to write, making visible a part of Jewish experience which otherwise would have been forgotten.

Lowenthal, Marvin, trans. *The Memoirs of Gluckel of Hameln*. New York: Schocken Books, 1989.

Rebecca Gratz (1781 - 1869)

This cup is dedicated to the memory of Rebecca Gratz, a woman whose educational and charitable endeavors helped to release other women and children from the burdens of poverty of the body and soul. Born in Philadelphia on March 4, 1781, Rebecca Gratz grew up in a large and loving family that always remained central to her life. An observant Jew who lived in the largely Christian elite society of nineteenth century Philadelphia, Gratz was a proud defender of Judaism. Her friendships with non-Jews gave her a forum for developing and expressing her ideas about the importance of religious tolerance in American society. Protective of poor Jews who were vulnerable to proselytizers, she joined women from her community to found the Female Hebrew Benevolent Society which provided food, fuel, shelter, and later an employment bureau and traveler's aid service. Gratz believed that women were uniquely responsible for the preservation of Jewish life in America. All the institutions she established were run by women, most notably the Hebrew Sunday School which provided Jewish women with the unprecedented opportunity to educate boys and girls in a religious context. Rebecca Gratz embodied her own statement that with "an unsubdued spirit" one can conquer all of life's difficulties. She forged a path that we continue to follow and honor through our own commitment to Jewish women's education, self-actualization and community.

Ashton, Dianne. *Rebecca Gratz: Women's Judaism in Antebellum America*. Wayne State University Press, 1997.

Rachel Kagan (1888 – ?)

With this cup, we honor Rachel Kagan, a woman who was dedicated to ensuring the rights and freedom of women in the newly founded State of Israel. Rachel Kagan, born in Odessa in 1888, was educated in secular and religious schools. She went on to study mathematics at the University of Odessa and Petrograd. In 1919, Kagan and her husband, Dr. Noah Cohen, immigrated to Palestine and settled in Haifa. Kagan was an outspoken member of the Union of Hebrew Women for Equal Rights in *Eretz Yisrael*, advocating tirelessly for women's suffrage. Kagan was also active in a nascent women's social service organization, working on behalf of needy families. With Hadassah women in the diaspora, she founded the Women's International Zionist Organization (WIZO) and was elected as its first president. In her capacity as president of WIZO, Rachel Kagan was one of two women to sign the Israeli Declaration of Independence. Kagan was elected to the first *Knesset* of the State of Israel as the sole representative of the women's party formed by WIZO and the Union of Hebrew Women for Equal Rights. Until her death, Rachel Kagan remained a sharp critic of modern Israel. She warned repeatedly that the country was not paying enough attention to bridging diverse ethnic groups, leveling economic disparities and educating its youth about the vision of their parents. She expressed deep frustration with a political system that prevented women from wielding significant influence.

Yishai, Yael. *Between the Flag and the Banner: Women in Israeli Politics*. Albany: State of University Press, 1997; Feuerstein, Emil. *Women Who Made History: 40 Portraits of Chalutzot in Eretz Israel*. Ministry of Defense, 1989.

Nehama Leibowitz (1905 – 1997)

With this cup we celebrate Nehama Leibowitz, a *Torah* scholar and teacher who helped countless Jews feel excited about their connection to the Jewish people. Nehama Leibowitz was born in 1905 in Riga. She earned a doctorate in Bible Studies from the University of Berlin and in 1931 she and her husband immigrated to Palestine. There she began teaching Bible at the Mizrachi Women's Teachers' Seminar in Jerusalem. Liebowitz transmitted to tens of thousands of students the value of the Bible in their everyday lives. She gave a weekly lesson over Israel Radio and distributed self-instruction study guides with questions about the weekly portion. Liebowitz's studies and study guides covering the entire *Torah* have been published and translated into English, French, Spanish and Dutch. In 1957, the year she joined the faculty of Tel Aviv University, Leibowitz was awarded the coveted Israel Prize for her contributions to education. In 1982, she received the Bialik Prize in Literature and Jewish Studies. An unpretentious woman, when she received an honorary doctorate from Bar-Ilan University, she remarked that she was pleased that a *Melamed*, a simple teacher, would be so honored. By the time Leibowitz died at the age of 92 on April 12, 1997, her influence and contributions were recognized by rabbis and scholars around the world. We raise our cup in honor of Nehama Leibowitz, a female pioneer, teacher and role model in the study of *Torah*, and we rededicate ourselves to continued learning.

"Nehama Liebowitz" Jerusalem Report. April 14 1997.

Rachel Luzzatto Morpurgo (1790 - 1871)

We honor Rachel Luzzatto Morpurgo, the first woman to write and publish modern Hebrew poetry. Rachel Luzzatto was born in Trieste in 1790 into a family of scholars and mystics. She was educated by her uncles who taught her not only Bible, commentaries and philosophy, but also the art of lithography. From an early age, she assisted them in the Luzzatto family printing business. And through her teens, quite unusual for a girl, she studied *Talmud* and subsequently, mystical texts. She also earned praise as a skillful seamstress, crafting all the clothes for three generations of women in her family. Despite her parents' wishes, Rachel Luzzatto refused many offers of marriage and waited until she was 29 to marry Jacob Morpurgo. The demands of managing a household and four small children made it difficult for her to write, and Jacob strongly disapproved of her scholarly activities. But she was determined to continue composing verses in celebration of family and community milestones, and she wrote late at night and on *Rosh Hodesh*, when women were traditionally exempted from housework. Morpurgo was honored by contemporary scholars who sought her literary opinion even though some confessed disbelief when they first discovered the gender of the poet whose rich Hebrew cadences they admired. Even her husband finally acknowledged her achievements with pride. As we bless this third cup, we remember Rachel Luzzatto Morpugo, a woman of spirit and skill, whose poetry transcends time, geography and personal circumstance.

Adelman, Howard. "Finding Women's Voices in Italian Jewish Literature" in Judith R. Baskin, ed. *Women of the Word: Jewish Women and Jewish Writing.* Detroit: Wayne State University Press, 1994.

Doña Gracia Nasi (1510-1569)

We remember "La Señora," "Ha-Giveret," Doña Gracia Nasi, who brought the children of Israel out from the burdens of secrecy and fear. Her birthname was Beatrice de Luna. Born 13 years after the Inquisition expelled all Jews from Portugal, Beatrice de Luna was raised by a prosperous Jewish family that chose to become Marranos—outwardly Christian, secretly Jews. Yet even as a young married woman, she began using her wealth and contacts to help other Marranos escape persecution. Rescue became her life's work. Although she was a successful businesswoman, Beatrice was arrested once and forced to relocate several times until she finally found safe haven under the protection of the Duke of Ferrara in Italy. There she took the name Gracia, (the equivalent of her Hebrew name Hannah) and at age 35, began to live openly as a Jew. She expanded both her business and rescue activities and became a renowned patron of Jewish letters. The Ferrara Bible, a 1553 translation from Hebrew to Spanish, is dedicated to "the Very Magnificent Lady" whose "merits have always earned her the most sublime place among our people."

Henry, S. and Taitz, E. *Written Out of History: Our Jewish Foremothers*. Fresh Meadows: Biblio Press, 1983; Slater, E. and R. *Great Jewish Women* New York: Jonathon David Publishers Inc., 1994.

Pauline M. Newman (1890? - 1986)

We raise this cup in honor of Pauline M. Newman. Pauline Newman was born to deeply religious parents in Kovno, Lithuania, sometime around 1890. In 1901, Newman's widowed mother immigrated to America with her children. Nine-year old Pauline went to work in a New York City hairbrush factory. Two years later, Pauline began working among other children in the "kindergarten" at the Triangle Shirtwaist Factory. Sixteen-year old Newman planned and led a rent strike involving 10,000 families in lower Manhattan. It was the largest rent strike New York City had yet seen, and it catalyzed decades of tenant activism that eventually led to the establishment of rent control. Once Newman's talent for organizing became apparent, the International Ladies' Garment Workers' Union hired her. For more than seventy years she worked for the Union as an organizer, labor journalist, health educator, and government liaison. An acerbic woman whose unorthodox tastes ran to cropped hair and tailored tweed jackets, Newman loved the labor movement. She referred to the ILGWU as her "family" and believed that it was, for all its flaws, the best hope for women garment workers. Newman's "family" also embraced a cross-class circle of women reformers that included Eleanor Roosevelt, Rose Schneiderman, and Frieda Miller, Newman's partner of 56 years. This circle of women shaped the body of laws and government protections that most workers now take for granted.

Orleck, Annelise. *Common Sense and a Little Fire: Women and Working-Class Politics 1900-1965*. Chapel Hill: University of North Carolina Press, 1995.

Bertha Pappenheim (1859 - 1936)

Raised in a wealthy Orthodox family in mid-19th century Vienna, Bertha Pappenheim was struck with paralysis after nursing her dying father through a long terminal illness. Under the care of Joseph Breuer, a colleague of Freud's, she devised a "talking cure" for herself, and as "Anna O," sparked the development of psychoanalysis. She then turned her extraordinary energies to the needs of other women. Infuriated by the disenfranchisement of women in the German Jewish community, she founded the *Judischer Frauenbund*, the first Jewish organization to fight for women's civil and religious rights. "The People of Book locked women out of Jewish spirituality," she said, and she considered the exclusion of Jewish women from learning a sin. To give the next generation of Jews greater access to their legacy, she translated the memoirs of one of her own ancestors, Glikl of Hameln. Deeply committed to social service, Pappenheim took as her lifelong cause the plight of homeless Jewish women. She travelled tirelessly through Eastern Europe, Greece and Turkey, visiting brothels where destitute Jewish women were forced to work. She consulted with doctors, social workers and the police. She campaigned strenuously among the male leadership of local Jewish communities, urging them to address the effects of poverty and social dislocation on Jewish women and their children. Issuing a bitter public report in 1904, Pappenheim rose to international prominence for her relief work and vocational education. In 1907, she founded *Isenberg*, Europe's first Jewish shelter and group home for single mothers and their children and for girls escaping prostitution. She ran this home base for what she called her "Sisyphus work" for 29 years, personally helping thousands of women.

Henry, S. and Taitz, E. *Written Out of History: Our Jewish Foremothers*. Fresh Meadows: Biblio Press, 1983; Slater, E. and R. *Great Jewish Women* New York: Jonathon David Publishers Inc., 1994.

Rose Schneiderman (1884-1972)

Eight-year-old Rose Schneiderman arrived in New York City from Poland in 1890 with her parents and three younger brothers. Five years later, Schneiderman was forced to quit school to support her family. Her first job in a department store demanded 64 hours of work for subsistence wages. It was as a sewing machine operator that Schneiderman organized the first woman's local of the Jewish socialist union, United Cloth, Hat, Cap and Millinery Workers. Through her forty-five year involvement as a leader of the Women's Trade Union League, Schneiderman organized countless strikes, trained young leaders, helped negotiate labor disputes and worked to establish continuing education programs for women workers. She was an extremely popular speaker who travelled throughout the country enlisting support for labor and women's suffrage. She ran for the United Stated Senate in 1920 and was the only woman appointed in Roosevelt's National Recovery Administration in 1933. Her influence, commitment and persistence were crucial in drafting and passing much of the legislation that has long been taken for granted by workers in this country, including: social security, worker's compensation, the elimination of child labor, maternity leave, safety laws, minimum wage and unemployment insurance. As we drink this cup, let us draw inspiration from Rose Schneiderman, who once proclaimed "what the working woman wants is the right to live, not simply exist. The worker must have bread, but she must have roses, too."

Orleck, Annelise. *Common Sense and a Little Fire: Women and Working-Class Politics 1900-1965*. Chapel Hill: University of North Carolina Press, 1995.

Manya Wilbushewitch Shochat (1880 - 1961)

We honor Manya Wilbushewitch Shochat. Manya Wilbushewitch, daughter of middle-class Russian Jewish parents, was first exposed to revolutionary ideas while working as a carpenter in her brother's factory in Minsk. Imprisoned in 1899 because of her contacts in revolutionary circles, she became convinced that a Jewish workers' movement would lead to an extension of Jewish civil rights. The charismatic, outspoken young woman participated in the founding of the Jewish Independent Labor Party, which collapsed a few years later in the wake of the Kishinev *pogrom*. Visiting Palestine in 1904, Shochat concluded that only through collective agricultural settlement could a class of Jewish workers emerge, a pre-condition for building a Jewish homeland. She returned to Palestine in 1907 to help establish the country's first ideologically-based cooperative agricultural settlement at Sejera. A year later, with Israel Shochat whom she later married, she helped found *HaShomer*, a network for the training and support of guards for the increasing number of Jewish settlements. When they extended their work to the creation of a Jewish militia, the Shochats were deported by Turkish authorities. Returning to Palestine in 1919, Manya and Israel Shochat devoted their energies to building the infrastructure of a workers' state.

In 1930, Shochat was among the founders of the League for Arab-Jewish Friendship. By the end of her life, the worker's settlements she envisioned had been realized in *kibbutzim* and *moshavim* across Israel.

Shazar, Rachel Katznelson, ed. *The Plough Woman: Memoirs of Pioneer Women of Palestine.* New York: Herzl Press, 1975.

Henrietta Szold (1860 - 1945)

With this cup we celebrate Henrietta Szold, a towering figure in 20th century history. Born into the German Jewish community in Baltimore in 1860, Henrietta Szold spent the first decades of her life under the tutelage of her father, an erudite European Rabbi. Under the *nom de plume* Shulamit, she published articles on Jewish life. Profoundly influenced by the Russian Jews who arrived in Baltimore in the 1880s, Szold opened a night school for immigrants and along with her father, joined one of the first Zionist study circles in America. After her father's death, Szold and her mother and sister moved to New York so that she could study at the Jewish Theological Seminary where she was accepted under the condition that she would not pursue a rabbinic diploma. She continued to work as the primary editor for the Jewish Publication Society while editing and translating manuscripts for Seminary faculty. In 1909, when she was close to fifty, she took her first trip to Palestine. On her return she founded Hadassah, a women's Zionist organization dedicated "to healing the body and soul" of the Jewish people. A brilliant organizer and educator, Szold spent the next decades of her life building a comprehensive health care and social welfare system in Palestine. In the final years of her life she directed Youth Aliyah, which helped to save and resettle close to 50,000 Jewish children from Nazi occupied Europe. As we raise this cup in honor of Henrietta Szold, we recall the charge she once gave a group of Hadassah women, "dare to dream—and when you dream, dream big."

Antler, Joyce, *The Journey Home: Jewish Women and the American Century.* Free Press, 1997.

Lillian D. Wald (1867- 1940)

We dedicate this cup to the memory of Lillian D. Wald who, throughout her life, stretched out her arms and heart in the service of creating a more just society for America's underprivileged. Born in Rochester, New York in 1867, Lillian D. Wald might have said that her life truly began twenty six years later, when as a young nurse, she visited a poor family in a crumbling tenement on the Lower East Side. The largely Jewish immigrant population was in dire need of affordable health care and Wald, through pioneering public health nursing, was going to offer it. During the next decades, Wald founded the Visiting Nurse Service of New York and the Henry Street Settlement, institutions that continue to improve the quality of life for residents of New York City today. Championing the causes of nursing, unionism, tenement reform, women's suffrage, child welfare, and antimilitarism, Wald became a major civic figure in local, national and international arenas. Her commitment to the health of individuals at home became increasingly connected to a concern for the health of nations throughout the world. As we bless this cup, we remember the legacy of Lillian Wald, drawing inspiration from this woman who remained throughout her life "consecrated to the saving of human life, the promotion of happiness and the expansion of good will among people."

"Lillian Wald" by Marjorie Feld in Hyman and Moore, eds. *Jewish Women in America: An Historical Encyclopedia.* New York: Routledge, 1997.

GLOSSARY

bat	daughter of
bat mitzvah	celebration of a daughter's taking on the responsibility of being an adult Jew
B'nei B'rak	town in both ancient and modern Israel
bima	literal (lit.) raised place; focal point of synagogue
b'racha, pl. b'rachot	blessing(s)
challah	traditional braided egg bread used as part of *Shabbat* celebration
chameitz	leaven; traditionally, all leavened grain, wheat, spelt, barley and rye and derivatives that are forbidden during the eight day celebration of Passover
cheider	lit. room; traditional religious school
dayeinu	lit. it would have been enough
haggadah	lit. telling; liturgy of the Passover *seder*
Hallel	lit. praise; liturgy from Psalms added to morning prayers on holidays
kadish	from the root k-d-sh, to sanctify or set apart; prayer of praise, honor, or memory
Kadish D'rabanan	lit. the Scholars' Praise; traditionally, prayer said after study
ketubah	traditional marriage document
kibbutzim, moshavim	collective agricultural settlements
kotel	the remaining segment of the western retaining wall of the Temple in Jerusalem
makom kadosh	lit. holy place
manna	food that sustained the Israelites in the desert
m'chitza	divider between men's and women's sections in traditional synagogues
mikvah	traditional Jewish ritual bath
midrashic	of, or pertaining to *midrashim*
midrashim	elaborations or interpretations of Biblical text (plural of *midrash*)
Mishna	legal codification containing the core of the Oral Law
Mitzrayim	lit. the narrows; Egypt
mitzva, pl. mitzvot	lit. commandment; Jewish laws traditionally understood as God's word; also interpreted as opportunity to increase holiness
Nisan	the Hebrew month in which Passover falls; the first *seder* is celebrated on the eve of the fifteenth of Nisan
rabbanit	(female) rabbi
Rosh Chodesh	lit. the head of the month; the first day of the Hebrew month when the new moon appears; a time that has traditionally been a semi-holiday for women
Sarai	wife of Abram; when God makes the covenant with Abram, Sarai becomes Sarah and Abram becomes Abraham to reflect their changed status as matriarch and patriarch of the Israelite people (Genesis 17:4ff)
seder	lit. order
Sefer Torah	scroll of the Five Books of Moses
Shabbat	lit. rest; Sabbath
Sh'china	lit. dwelling or indwelling presence; Divine Presence, often understood as the feminine manifestation of God.
Sh'ma	central prayer in daily liturgy: "Hear O Israel, God is our God, God is One"
sh'tei f'amim	lit. two times
Talmud	compilation of *Mishnah* and *Gemara* (commentary and supplement to *Mishnah*)
tikkun olam	lit. repair of the world
Torah	broadly, Jewish law and learning; specifically, the first five books of the Bible
tzedaka	lit. justice work; charity
Ya Sh'china	two names of God linked together
Y'rushalayim	Jerusalem

NOTES AND SOURCES

This *haggadah*, prepared under the auspices of Ma'yan, represents the work of several hands and hearts over the years. The primary authors of *The Journey Continues* are the editors: Tamara Cohen, Rabbi Sue Levi Elwell, Debbie Friedman, and Ronnie M. Horn. Particular pieces are attributed below. Thanks to Coraline Dahlin, Barbara Dobkin, Eve Landau, and Ruth Silverman. Thanks, also, to Joyce Antler, Kathy Barr, Ayelet Cohen, Randee Friedman, Gwynn Kessler, Benay Lappe, Rabbi Carol Levithan, Rabbi Joy Levitt, Nurit Shein, Rabbi David Sulomm Stein.

Songs

B'ruchot Habaot ©1988 Deborah Lynn Friedman
The Time is Now ©1996 Deborah Lynn Friedman and Tamara Ruth Cohen
Light These Lights ©1995 Deborah Lynn Friedman
The Journey Song ©1995 Deborah Lynn Friedman and Tamara Ruth Cohen
Mi Shebeirach ©1988 Deborah Lynn Friedman and D'rora Setel

L'chi Lach based on Genesis 12:1-2 © 1988 Deborah Lynn Friedman and Savina Teubal
Kadish D'rabanan © 1988 Deborah Lynn Friedman
Miriam's Song based on Exodus 15:20-21 ©1988 Deborah Lynn Friedman
B'chol Dor Vador from Haggadah © 1996 Deborah Lynn Friedman
Birkat Hamazon based on traditional text ©1996 Deborah Lynn Friedman
Hodu based on Psalm 118:1-2 © 1981 Deborah Lynn Friedman
T'fillat Haderech based on traditional text © 1998 Deborah Lynn Friedman
All songs above: © Deborah Lynn Friedman (ASCAP), Sounds Write Productions, Inc. (ASCAP)

Mir'yam Han'viah ©1989 Leila Gal Berner. Conceived by Rabbi Leila Gal Berner and Rabbi Arthur Waskow; Hebrew by Leila Gal Berner. This song originally appeared in *Or Chadash*, a shabbat morning siddur published by P'nai Or Religious Fellowship. Used by permission of author.

Intoduction ©1997 Sue Levi Elwell
"Theology and Blessings" includes insights of Rachel Adler in Elwell, Sue Levi, ed. *And We Were All There: A Feminist Passover Haggadah*. Los Angeles: American Jewish Congress Feminist Center, 1994.
B'dikat Chameitz "Searching for leaven: a new approach" ©1998 Tamara Ruth Cohen
Creating Holy Space "To the Temple in Jerusalem" ©1996 Tamara Ruth Cohen
T'chine for candle lighting adapted by Nurit Shein and Sue Levi Elwell from a traditional Sephardic *t'chine* found in Cohen, Jonathan, ed. *The Sephardi Haggadah*. Jerusalem: Feldheim Publishers, 1988.
Kos Miryam based on ©1992 Kol Ishah, PO Box 132, Wayland MA, 01778. May be used, but not sold, by notifying Kol Ishah in writing. Please include this copyright on all copies.
"How does the journey to freedom begin" ©1995 Tamara Ruth Cohen
Karpas ©1995 Ronnie M. Horn
Yachatz ©1996 Tamara Ruth Cohen
Magid *Ha Lachma Anya*, *The Four Daughters*, *Tzei Ul'mad*, The Plagues, *Dayeinu*, ©1996 Tamara Ruth Cohen
The Four Questions, "Only God..", *Ma-aseh*: It is told...", *Mit'chila* In the beginning, ©1996 Ronnie M. Horn
Maror ©1995 Tamara Ruth Cohen
Tzafun ©1995, *Sh'foch Chamatcha* ©1996 Ronnie M. Horn
Nirtza ©1995 Tamara Ruth Cohen
Four Cups 1999: Written by Susan Sapiro and Tamara Cohen. See: Hyman and Moore, eds. *Jewish Women in America: An Historical Encyclopedia*. New York: Routledge, 1997.